WOMEN IN CRIMINAL JUSTICE

True Cases *By & About*
Canadian Women
& the Law

Other Books in Durvile's 'True Cases' Series

~ Book One ~

Tough Crimes
True Cases by Top Canadian Criminal Lawyers (2014)
Editors: C.D. Evans and Lorene Shyba

Authors: Edward L. Greenspan, Richard Wolson, Marilyn Sandford, Earl Levy, Peter Martin, John Rosen, Fred Ferguson, William Smart, Richard Peck, Noel O'Brien, Joel Pink, Patrick Fagan, Brian Beresh, Mark Brayford, Marie Henein, C.D. Evans, William Trudell, John Vertes, Thomas Dalby, Hersh Wolch

Paperback: ISBN 978-0-9947352-5-6
E-book: 978-0-9952322-2-8 Audiobook: 978-0-9689754-8-0

~ Book Two ~

Shrunk: Crime and Disorders of the Mind
True Cases by Forensic Psychologists and Psychiatrists (2016)
Foreword: Dr. Lisa Ramshaw
Editors: Dr. Lorene Shyba and Dr. J. Thomas Dalby

Authors: J. Thomas Dalby, Sven A. Christianson, Patrick Baillie, Jack White, Joel Watts, Louise Olivier, Stephen Porter, Tianna Dilley, Donald Dutton, Barry Cooper, Jacqueline Kanipayur, Marc Nesca, Jeffrey Waldman, Lawrence Ellerby, Richard D. Schneider, David Dawson, William Trudell

Paperback: ISBN 978-0-9947352-0-1
E-book: 978-0-9947352-3-2, Audiobook: 978-0-9952322-7-3

~ Book Three ~

More Tough Crimes
True Cases by Canadian Judges and Criminal Lawyers (2017)
Foreword: Hon. Patrick LeSage
Editors: William Trudell and Lorene Shyba

Donald Bayne, Brian H. Greenspan, David Bright, Mona Duckett, Brock Martland, Faith Finnestad, Brian Beresh, Breese Davies, Jonathan Rudin, Alan D. Gold, James Lockyer, James Ogle, Clayton Rice, Raymond Wyant, Joseph Di Luca, William Trudell

Paperback: ISBN 978-0-9947352-0-1
E-book: 978-0-9947352-3-2, Audiobook: 978-0-9952322-7-3

~ Upcoming, Book Five ~

True Cases in the Digital Age: Law and Technology (2019)
Editors: William Trudell and Lorene Shyba

Paperback: ISBN 978-1-988824-19-2
E-book: 978-1-988824-20-8, Audiobook: 978-1-988824-21-5

WOMEN IN CRIMINAL JUSTICE

True Cases *By* & *About* Canadian Women & *the* Law

FOREWORD BY

The Right Honourable Beverley McLachlin

EDITED BY

William Trudell and Lorene Shyba

DURVILE PUBLICATIONS

Calgary, Alberta, Canada

Durvile Publications Ltd.

Calgary, Alberta, Canada
www.durvile.com

National Library of Canada
Cataloguing in Publications Data
Trudell, William and Shyba, Lorene

Women in Criminal Justice: True Cases By and About Canadian Women and the Law
Issued in print and electronic formats
ISBN 978-0-994735-24-9 (print pbk) | 978-1-988824-14-7 (e-book)
ISBN: 978-1-988824-15-4 (audiobook)

1. True Crime —collections
2. Gender and the Law
3. Canadian Law
4. Criminal Law
5. Canadian Essays—21st Century

I. Trudell, William, editor
II. Shyba, Lorene Mary, editor

Book Four in the True Cases Series

Cover photo of "Ivsticia" by D. Gordon E. Robertson

We would like to acknowledge the support of the Alberta Government through the Alberta Book Fund.

Durvile is a member of the Book Publishers Association of Alberta (BPAA) and Association of Canadian Publishers (ACP).

Printed in Canada at Houghton Boston Printing, Saskatoon.

First edition, first printing. 2018

To my wife Jennifer, and my daughters Eryn and Clara and grandaughters Yoko and Chelsea. They light up my life.

— William Trudell

To my wonderful partner David and my brave and handsome sons Austin and Warwick.

— Lorene Shyba

Contents

Contents

"The female ascendancy and the end of the old boy network was by far the most significant revolutionary transformation of my profession."

— *C.D. Evans QC*
Less Painful Duties:
Reflections on the Revolution in the Legal Profession

"When I'm sometimes asked, 'When will there be enough women on the [US] Supreme Court?' And I say, 'When there are nine,' people are shocked. But there'd been nine men, and nobody's ever raised a question about that."

— *Ruth Bader Ginsberg*
Associate Justice of the Supreme Court of the United States

Photo: Roy Grogan

Foreword

The Right Honourable Beverley McLachlin

Five decades ago, the Canadian criminal justice system was a man's world. Police, prosecutors, defence lawyers, judges — all, down to a man — were male. Women appeared in cameo roles as victims and accused persons, to be sure. But the people running the show and determining the outcomes were all men.

Fast forward fifty years and the picture is very different. Women are part of every part of the criminal process. They are policewomen. They are prosecutors. They are defence lawyers. They are judges. Women still appear in their roles of victim and accused, but the stereotypes of the victim who 'asked for it' and the accused who is a 'bad woman' have been banished. No longer do men pull all the strings and determine all the outcomes.

The presence of women in the Canadian justice system has changed the system in important ways. It has provided reassurance to women called to testify or answer for their deeds before our courts; no longer do women standing up before the court look around and feel themselves not only outnumbered and outgunned, but confronting an alien world. It has brought new, female perspectives into the criminal justice system. Finally, it has produced a group of women who are going beyond the courtroom and sharing their experiences in the criminal justice system with the public.

This book attests to all three benefits. It describes and affirms the presence of women in the criminal justice system. It offers a host of unique perspectives into the working of the system and how it impacts women in all their diverse roles. And its existence is an example of women moving beyond the courtroom to enrich the public's understanding of criminal justice in Canada.

The insights offered in this volume fall into three broad categories — what it is like to be a woman working in the justice system as a lawyer or judge; what it is like to be a woman caught up in the justice system, as a victim or as an accused person; and how we can change the system to make it fairer to the people — women and men — it impacts. Since the stories are told by women working in the justice system who are passionate about the people they deal with and about justice, the three types of insight often merge.

The first set of insights is concerned with what it is like to be a woman working in the justice system as lawyer or judge. Among the chapters, Danielle Côté writes movingly of the judge haunted by the fear that the person she has convicted may not, in the end, be guilty, "I am always alone with the burden of my decision, with only myself to blame if an error is made." Jennifer Briscoe provides a fascinating description of being a prosecutor in a 'fly-in team,' meting out justice in remote Arctic communities — of the remarkable people she met, "the cold … the silent darkness, and the heavenly galaxies that … carve into and shape your spiritual connection to the earth." Jill Presser shares the anxiety of a mother torn between staying with her child and going to court, and how her conflicting emotions are resolved by her daughter's note after she has won a landmark case, "I am proud of you and hope to do something as meaningful with my life as you have done with yours." Lucie Joncas tells us of her anguish as she struggles to come to terms with the suicide of a mentally ill client. Iona Jaffe recounts the burdens of a prosecutor in a terrorism offence. And Jennifer Trehearne shares the burden of a client dead in prison after she failed to secure his bail.

The second set of insights focuses on how the criminal justice system impacts and shapes women who find themselves caught up in it. Among these chapters, Nancy Morrison describes her role as a judge in a case of long-running family-abetted sexual abuse of a young girl who refused to accept the wrongs done to her and courageously pursued justice for herself and others like her. Catherine Dunn shares the story of a young First Nations mother charged with failing to provide medical assistance to her dying daughter, through the lens of the woman's experiences as the victim of domestic abuse and her domestic partner's experiences of residential schools. Kaysi Fagan describes the dilemma of fashioning an appropriate sentence for an aging woman convicted of a serious drug offence in "Weeding out the Good." And Susan Lang recounts stories of mothers wrongfully found to be alcohol and drug abusers because of invalid laboratory tests, with tragic consequences for them and the children that were taken away from them.

The third set of insights that emerges from these essays concerns failings in the criminal justice system and how we can rectify them. Included in these insights, Susan Lang recounts the havoc that bad science has wreaked in criminal courts: "We must remember that science is a tool, not a solution." Catherine Dunn tells us that "children and vulnerable adults … need to be more supported in the justice system," and urges more alcohol treatment centres and more assistance to Indigenous people struggling with alcohol and drug addictions. Deborah Hatch tells us that legal aid, indispensable to a fair criminal justice system, is in crisis, and warns, "The liberty of … accused persons is being sacrificed while debates continue as to how and by whom legal aid should be funded." Karen Hudson recounts the promising steps being taken in Nova Scotia to improve the criminal justice system. And Lucie Joncas and Jennifer Trehearne underline the need to deal with mental illness in the criminal courtroom more compassionately and more effectively.

The reader emerges from reading *Women in Criminal Justice* with two pictures in mind. The first picture consists of vivid images of what actually goes on in Canada's criminal courtrooms. There is justice to be found there, but too often injustice as well. And despite the progress that has been made, too often it is the vulnerable in our society — women, Indigenous persons, the mentally ill — who are the victims of lack of legal aid, sloppy science, and lack of appropriate sentencing alternatives. The second picture is of a cadre of people like the women who contributed to this book, who work without respite to achieve just outcomes for the people they deal with, often in the face of difficulty and at considerable personal cost. Both pictures are part of the justice system; both are important.

— The Right Honourable Beverley McLachlin
17th Chief Justice of Canada (2000 – 2017)

Lorene Shyba

Introduction

Bill Trudell and I approached the editing and publication of this book with a mutual aim; to create a volume for Durvile's True Cases series wherein Canadian women judges and criminal lawyers tell about cases from their careers that they found particularly challenging. The stories that emerged have amazed us with their compassionate perspectives on urgent issues of our times — sexual assault, Indigenous, child protection and motherhood issues, mental health and suicide, LGBTQ+, immigration, drugs, and terrorism. Although some authors chose to write about high-profile cases, the lion's share of chapters focus on matters of social and personal impact.

Women in Criminal Justice was Bill's brainchild and I supported his bright idea all the way. We started working on it in early 2017, pulling our nucleus of writers together well before the entertainment industry-driven #MeToo and #TimesUp empowerment campaigns. It is a point of pride to clarify that we did not join a women's rights bandwagon, rather, we initiated and are now delivering a unique project that is making heard the voices of fascinating women from the legal profession.

As a glimpse of the book's development, we originally tried out snappy titles like 'Skirts', which was intended to be a gender-influenced play on the television series *Suits*, but the novelty of our 'Skirts' title was short-lived (although it would have made a great hashtag campaign). After 'Skirts', we auditioned the titles 'Silk' or 'Silks' and even designed a book cover and a promotional campaign around the theme. However for reasons that seem strange to a non-lawyer such as myself, most provinces in Canada bestow Queen's Council (QC) barrister honourifics, aka 'taking silk', but Ontario and Quebec no longer grant the honour. Judges, by virtue of their silk gowns in every jurisdiction, would have fit the title, but the disconnect with 'Silks' and Ontario/Quebec lawyers was difficult to reconcile. *Women in Criminal Justice* had been our subtitle all along and so we elevated it to top billing.

As we began hearing story pitches from contributors, a few differences became apparent in comparison to Durvile's previous True Cases books. Authors' themes focused on many new topics, such as legal aid and personal stories of balancing home with work, instead of concentrating on brilliant courtroom strategies or winning a big case. Even when stories were about big cases with huge stakes, such as Iona Jaffe's story about the Toronto 18 terrorists or Deborah Hatch's recounting of the Wendy Scott case, *Women in Criminal Justice* authors stepped up to share personal reflections, often in a highly subjective and empathetic mode.

Many authors shared nuanced and private inner thoughts — something I had seldom seen before among the male writers in previous volumes. These amusing and intimate inner thoughts are typeset throughout the book in italics, ranging from Barbara Jackman thinking, *Were [the judges] afraid that if they made a mistake it could result in others coming to harm?*, Kim Pate wondering, *How serious could the risk be that the women [rioting in prison] posed if the head of security believed a baby could calm the situation?*, to musings of a currently unidentified author who thought, *What the fuck am I doing? How did we get here?*

A Unique Experience in Production

Collecting stories together for a book can be a pretty big job. It was not any easier to get authors to submit stories on deadline than it has been in previous True Cases anthologies, maybe harder than ever if truth be told, but the reasons for tardiness were more varied. We heard the usual, such as, "This trial is dragging on and I'm swamped," or "I have back-to-back murder cases and can't get to writing until [whenever]," but sprinkled into the mix were never-heard-before reasons like, "I'm having a baby next week," and "I have to fly down to the retirement village again to be with my mom." The most heartbreaking justification for lateness involved a rough session of chemotherapy.

Another interesting difference with this group is that instead of corresponding with executive assistants during business hours, as has mostly been the case with other books in the series, I had direct contact with authors. We collaborated on corrections and improvements to stories on an hourly basis as deadlines loomed, and at all times of night and day through multiple time zones. My admiration for these women has grown from respect into genuinely liking them.

Revisiting the matter of the unidentified author whose 'f-bomb' private musing rocks the top of this page, this special person also insinuated that we "forced her" to write a chapter. Yes, it is true, we twisted her arm some, in spite of being threatened with permanent expulsion from her organ donation list. We were tempted to edit out the incendiary "forced to" words from the first sentence of her chapter, but are not embarrassed to admit that, indeed, we did bully her a bit.

Like many of the other authors who we 'asked nicely' to write, Rosellen Sullivan is a brilliant and compassionate criminal defence lawyer. But over and above that, she practices in

St. John's and with her participation, we have coast-to-coast-to-coast Canadian representation. This starts in British Columbia with Nancy Morrison, who also represents Saskatchewan, having grown up in Yorkton, and continues with writers from all across the country ending up with Karen Hudson from Nova Scotia and, of course, Rosellen from Newfoundland and Labrador. The far North is represented by Jennifer Briscoe's story, taking place, as it does, in Whitehorse, Yellowknife, Taloyoak, Old Crow, and Nunavut's "big smoke" of Iqaluit.

Hard Work and Just Outcomes

As The Right Honourable Beverley McLachlin points out in the foreword to this book, story insights develop around several themes including how it feels to be a woman working in the justice system, how the criminal justice system impacts and shapes women who find themselves caught up in it, and failings in the criminal justice system and how we can rectify them. In addition, Justice McLachlin's point about how hard women work in the justice system work can be applied to women in many other areas of professional endeavour.

If I may use my own life as an example, when I was a girl in Calgary, I was told I could be anything I wanted to be. I knuckled down Alberta style and did exactly that — in fields of media and communications rather than on the farm, or in the justice system, but these were challenging careers nonetheless. When I went back to graduate school after I'd raised my kids, certain professors informed me that women are "oppressed within a social construction called a patriarchal hegemony." Not to seem a dolt but, *How had I not known that?*

Not realizing that men were supposedly better than women was likely the best thing that happened to me because I seldom felt inferior, let alone oppressed. I was amidst a wave of Canadian women who carved out and excelled at careers of our choice because we apparently didn't know any better. (Thinking back on it now, and in the light of Justice McLachlin's comments,

I am sure that like my sisters who chose the legal profession, I work harder than most of the guys.)

In addition to thanking the Rt. Hon. Beverley McLachlin and all the *Women in Criminal Justice* authors for their brilliant writing and hard work, there is another group of writers who we would like to thank. On behalf of editors Bill Trudell, C.D. Evans, and J. Thomas Dalby, I thank the amazing women who have contributed to the True Cases series in previous books — Marie Henein and Marilyn Sandford in *Tough Crimes*; Lisa Ramshaw and Louise Olivier in *Shrunk*; and Faith Finnestad, Breese Davies, and Mona Duckett in *More Tough Crimes.*

Many women in *Women in Criminal Justice* and the other True Cases books have written about problems that their clients have had in a man's world — especially troubling are the cases of domestic violence and sexual assault. I have seen examples of disturbances of this nature many times in the pages of the True Cases books, and they have always been emotionally hard to bear. I am greatly impressed that the thoughtful women lawyers, judges, and mental health experts who have written for us are in a position to advocate and implement solutions to correct these kinds of inequities. Setting words into action is an ongoing endeavour among writers throughout the entire series.

There are several design elements in the book that bear explanation. On the cover is the statue of Justicia (Ivstica), created in 1912 by sculptor Walter Allward for a memorial to King Edward VII. The plaster casts of Justicia and her sibling Veritas languished in a government storage vault for fifty years before being cast in bronze to grace the entrance doors of the Supreme Court of Canada building. Our Justicia is not blindfolded like most depictions of the Lady of Justice, nor does she hold forth a sword and scales. Instead, she shows compassionate and level determination in her eyes and keeps her sword well-sheathed. It occurs to me that she would be a good listener.

Another graphic element that runs throughout the book

Design elements in this book: Women's and Gender Studies Department logo of the University of Saskatchewan, created by Joan Relke; and Justica (Ivstica) from the entrance of the Supreme Court of Canada building in Ottawa, Walter Allward sculptor.

is the Women's and Gender Studies (WGSt) logo from the University of Saskatchewan. This beautiful and dynamic logo was designed and donated to the WGSt Department by artist Joan Relke. In the department's words, the design, "Combines the symbol for woman with the sun-moon symbol for male-female, mirroring a balance between genders." The plant imagery lower-portion of this logo has also been used as a graphic element to divide chapters.

If I have to give a man the last word, I cannot think of anyone I would rather share these pages with than Bill Trudell, especially given that he is praising 'the Oracle'. He says

> In the beginning of my career, I had the privilege of Articling and practicing for my first three years at Osler Hoskin in Toronto. I had the unique honour to meet, indeed work with, someone affectionately referred to as 'the Oracle'. In the corner office was the remarkable Bertha Wilson. She meant so much to so many and guided innumerable careers, mine included. I likely had an inflated opinion of my own importance as one day in my second year, I knocked on her door in my campaign to try to practice Criminal Law at the Large Firm. I submitted that Large Firms should establish Criminal Law

> Departments to become full service, if you will. I told her that I would like to pursue that path, with supervision of course. There was an awful silence and then she looked across the desk at me and in that incredible Scottish voice said this, "Ah, William, I think you're brilliant...but I haven't seen it yet!"
>
> For over forty years, I still hear that cherished voice every time I think I've accomplished something. When I thought of this book, I think I had Bertha Wilson in mind, that amazing trailblazer and first woman appointed to our Supreme Court. I wish now I could walk down to her office and show her *Women in Criminal Justice,* not to revisit her opinion of me but to thank her. I believe she would have been so very proud of Lorene and all the women herein who I am sure have been inspired by her, as was I.

Bill and I sincerely hope you enjoy reading this book as much as we have enjoyed working on it.

— Lorene Shyba
Publisher, Durvile Publications
and co-editor True Cases Series

The Women in Criminal Justice

The Honourable Susan Lang received her law degree from Osgoode Hall Law School. She conducted an Independent Review relating to forensic hair testing for drugs by the Motherisk Drug Testing Laboratory. Before that she served nine years on the Court of Appeal for Ontario and fifteen years on the Superior Court, including as Regional Senior Judge for Toronto. Her contributions were recognized by an honourary Doctor of Laws from the Law Society of Upper Canada.

Hon. Susan Lang

Flawed Forensic Evidence

The Motherisk Hair Analysis Independent Review

In late 2014, I was asked by the Government of Ontario whether I would be interested in conducting an independent review of what turned out to be hair testing being conducted by the Motherisk Drug Testing Laboratory (the Lab) located at the renowned Hospital for Sick Children. The Lab's hair test results were being used in criminal and child protection cases purportedly to establish whether a parent was taking drugs of abuse or alcohol. Initially, I thought it unlikely I would take on this task since I had retired not long before to pursue other interests but, as soon as I was informed of the context, I knew I would say yes.

Hair Testing Gone Wrong

An Ontario mother of two girls adamantly denied that she was a drinker, let alone a chronic abuser of alcohol. She gave this denial to a child protection worker who was investigating her ability to parent. At the request of the worker, the Lab tested the mother's hair and gave the opinion that the mother was a chronic alcohol abuser. The Children's Aid Society removed both children, then ages nine and thirteen, from their home and placed them in foster care. Three years later, the mother was able to establish that she did not abuse alcohol. She did this by wearing an ankle bracelet that monitored her alcohol intake through her skin for a three-month period. She also gave the Lab a hair sample representing the same three-month period. The bracelet established that the mother was not drinking. The Lab's hair tests came back positive.

When told of the conflicting results, the Lab manager acknowledged that the Lab's preliminary test results were in error. A second, more sophisticated test established that the mother did not abuse alcohol. The Lab's flawed analysis and interpretation likely gave false positives in this and other cases. Among other problems, the Lab did not take into account the effect of the use of ethanol-containing hair products. Ethanol (alcohol) is a common ingredient in many hair products, including hair spray.

Within days of the corrected opinion, the Children's Aid Society ended its involvement with the family. Nevertheless, when the youngest girl returned to her mother's care she suffered from severe anxiety problems. As the child recalled, she had been moved through nine foster homes during her first year in care. The story of what happened to this family was identified during a subsequent joint investigation by the *Toronto Star* and CBC's *The Current* and *The Fifth Estate.*

Science, done badly, had failed many. Some parents and children lost contact with each other as a result of the flawed 'expert' opinion evidence emanating from the well-regarded laboratory at the highly respected Hospital for Sick Children in Toronto, often referred to as SickKids. More than one person was convicted criminally. For more than fifteen years, the justice system in Ontario failed to identify the unreliability of those opinions. This was not the first time that the justice system has been misled by unreliable scientific evidence. Once again, science had failed us.

The controversy about hair tests came to light only when *R. v. Broomfield* reached the Court of Appeal for Ontario in 2014.

The Broomfield Case

In August 2005, Ms. Broomfield's two-and-a-half year old toddler began suffering seizures. The child was transferred to SickKids.

In addition to several fractures of varying ages, SickKids identified potentially lethal amounts of cocaine in the child's bodily fluids. The cocaine caused the seizures. The child was treated and was eventually released from hospital, although with serious long-lasting consequences. At the time and throughout, Ms. Broomfield said that her child's ingestion of a dangerous level of cocaine reflected a single accidental incident.

Several days after the child's treatment, the Hospital collected samples of the child's hair for testing and analysis by its Motherisk Drug Testing Laboratory. While bodily fluid tests can only identify the presence of drug ingested within the past hours or perhaps days, hair testing can provide information about longer-term use. This is because drug incorporates into the hair and evidence of drug will remain as the hair grows. On average, and speaking very generally, hair grows at a rate of one centimeter a month so that, in theory, a hair test can give information about drugs for the number of months represented by the length of the hair sample.

The Broomfield fourteen-centimeter sample of hair would have represented roughly fourteen months of growth. After testing that sample, the Lab gave its opinion that the child had ingested large amounts of cocaine over the duration of the fourteen months preceding his admission.

Five days later, Ms. Broomfield was charged with several criminal counts, including aggravated assault (the cocaine ingestion leading to the seizures) and administering a noxious substance (cocaine) to her child allegedly over the preceding months. If the hair tests results were reliable, this would belie her explanation of an accidental ingestion leading to the medical emergency.

At Broomfield's 2009 trial, Dr. Gideon Koren, the Director of the Lab, testified that the results indeed established that her child had ingested substantial amounts of cocaine over fourteen months. Mr. Joey Gareri, the Lab's manager since 2005, had given similar evidence at the 2007 preliminary inquiry. Ms. Broomfield was convicted of the two cocaine-related charges. She was also convicted of other counts relating to the child's broken bones and her failure to have them treated.

The Broomfield Appeal

Ms. Broomfield appealed. She abandoned her appeal relating to the child's fractures, but pursued her appeal of the cocaine-related convictions.

On the appeal, Ms. Broomfield's appeal counsel, James Lockyer, tendered fresh evidence that was not available at trial. That evidence came from an expert toxicologist, Dr. Craig Chatterton. Dr. Chatterton had developed an expertise in forensic toxicology with a keen interest in hair analysis and interpretation. He moved to Canada from England in 2011 and became Deputy Chief Toxicologist at the Office of the Medical Examiner in Edmonton, Alberta.

At the time of the appeal, I believe Dr. Chatterton was the only expert in Canada with the knowledge and experience to give an opinion about the reliability of the hair testing done at the Motherisk Lab. He was critical of the Lab's methodology at each step of the hair testing. Both the Lab's director and its manager defended the Lab's methodology maintaining confidence in its reliability.

Based on the fresh evidence critical of the Lab's work, the Court of Appeal for Ontario concluded that there was a "genuine controversy" about the Lab's science and methodology. Since that evidence had not been available to the trial judge, the Court quashed the cocaine-related convictions. The Crown did not seek to proceed with a new trial. To do so, noted the Court, would not be in the interests of justice because Ms. Broomfield had already served the equivalent of a 49-month sentence on the fracture-related convictions.

The justice system was left with the Court of Appeal finding of a "genuine controversy" about the hair testing with no answer to that controversy in sight. Concern was widespread because child protection agencies (as well as a few parents) had used the Lab's hair test results in thousands of child protection cases in the preceding years and were continuing to do so.

Although SickKids continued to defend its Lab and its results, legislators, child protection agencies, family and criminal lawyers, individuals and investigative journalists began to ask questions —particularly and initially, the *Toronto Star*.

The controversy about the toxicology work done by the Lab was reminiscent of the case involving a pediatric pathologist, Dr. Charles Smith, also a purportedly pre-eminent expert from SickKids. In that case, the Goudge Report, released in 2008, detailed how flawed forensic pathology evidence had resulted in a number of wrongful criminal convictions. Was it conceivable that flawed expert evidence could be coming from another expert at the same Hospital at roughly the same time?

Child Protection and Science

I return to 2014, when the Government of Ontario asked me if I was interested in conducting an independent review of the Motherisk Lab. As mentioned, I had thought it unlikely that I would accept at the time, but upon reflection, I realized it fit very well with my years in the law. I have always had a great interest both in child protection and in science and its uses.

With this combination of interests at issue, I knew I would take on the Motherisk challenge.

Back in 1976 when I embarked on the practice of law, my partner Patricia Graham and I opened an all-women's law firm, which was quite a novelty. In retrospect, it was also brave. We did criminal, civil and family work — as well as virtually any other work that came through our door. From the early days, my work included child protection.

I came to know and represent families involved in child protection cases and developed a particular interest in representing grandparents who sought to care for their grandchildren as an alternative to foster care. I argued strenuously, not often successfully, that children are usually better kept in, rather than removed from, community.

In 1989, I was appointed a judge in the trial courts. In that capacity, I sat in different areas of the law, largely civil and criminal. While family law, including child protection, was not part of the Court's jurisdiction at that time, I always maintained a keen interest and deep appreciation for those of us who face difficult struggles and challenges in raising our children, particularly the vulnerable and marginalized among us. That vulnerability often arises from mental health issues, addictions, poverty and lack of family and other supports.

Over the course of my years as a trial judge, I developed a strong interest in trials that involved scientific evidence, beginning when I presided on the first HIV-related civil trial in Canada, which was one-year long. I also presided over a number of other less-lengthy trials involving medical malpractice, or engineering, or other aspects of scientific endeavours. Subsequently, I also heard appeals related to scientific issues during my nine very interesting years on the Court of Appeal for Ontario, before I retired from the bench in 2013.

That background, combined with learning about

Broomfield, prompted me to accept what I consider to be the significant honour of leading the Motherisk Hair Testing Review.

Strength of Belief in Reliability

I already had a great respect for everyone in the system of child protection, including the social workers, the lawyers and the judiciary, all of whom worked with dedication to identify what was best for children and to balance their safety with their attachment to family. Identifying that balance is not easy, and getting it wrong can have serious consequences. Protection workers work hard to decide on the best course. A decision whether to remove a child from a home is often a judgment call. Children removed from families are not always placed in idyllic foster care en route to a successful adoption.

When hair-test results first became available, those in the child protection field must have received them with gratitude and relief, particularly given their seemingly reliable source, coming as they did from the pre-eminent SickKids Hospital. The Hospital's reputation gave credibility and reliability to the Lab's hair test methodology. Social workers and the Courts believed they could use hair-test results to tell them whether a parent was taking drugs and in what quantities. Such results would serve the ancillary purpose of detecting whether the parent had lied about their use of drugs or alcohol. If they were perceived to have lied about drug or alcohol abuse, their credibility would be at serious risk on all matters.

The strength of belief in the legitimacy of the hair tests, and the lack of resources to challenge them, contributed to the lengthy delay in exposing their unreliability. Indeed, during much of this period, there was not even an expert in Canada able to do so.

Scope of the Motherisk Review

The Motherisk Review mandate covered the Lab's hair testing methodology from 2005 until 2015. I was required to report by December 15, 2015. The question before me was one of science and its application. If I found the methodology unreliable, I was asked to make recommendations about whether a further review should be conducted into the individual cases affected by the testing.

I accepted the Review knowing that I would have a legal team led by the highly regarded Linda Rothstein, who had extensive experience in commissions of inquiry. She was joined by Assistant Counsel Rob Centa, Tina Lie and later Jodi Martin. The legal team was sterling.

The Review engaged two accomplished forensic toxicologists: Dr. Gail Cooper, a highly experienced forensic toxicologist in Scotland, and Professor Olaf Drummer, an expert in forensic pharmacology and toxicology in Australia. They provided exceptional scientific expertise. Most importantly, from my perspective, they were great communicators — with each other and with the Review. They were in contact regularly over different time zones sorting through the data and other material received from the Lab.

When the Review was first announced, we knew it was going to take some time for the legal team to complete the necessary groundwork. While the team began document identification and obtained the necessary production from the Hospital and Lab, my husband and I took a scheduled trip to Australia and New Zealand to visit grandchildren. While in Australia, I took the opportunity to meet with Professor Drummer at his forensic lab and he also arranged for me to tour a forensic lab in New Zealand. In addition, I took the opportunity to meet with members of the judiciary and counsel familiar with the admissibility of forensic testing in their jurisdictions. This gave me a helpful start in beginning to appreciate the scientific and legal concepts that would be engaged by the Review. Our scientists continued this when they attended in Toronto to explain the science of hair testing and the methodology employed by the Lab. With their help, I came to appreciate the extent of what had gone wrong at the Lab and why.

In the meantime, the legal team in Toronto began receiving what eventually became thousands of documents from SickKids. The team randomly selected sample case files for each of the drugs and for alcohol to be reviewed by our scientists. The information included raw data used to generate the results, at least to the extent that the Lab had that data available. The Hospital also provided information about what oversight, or lack of oversight, it provided to the Lab. Based on the paper productions, the Review identified and interviewed the key individuals, either in person or by written question and answer.

We also consulted with many organizations including ones involved in forensics, healthcare, child protection, child advocacy, family and criminal law, academia and relevant government ministries. We examined reported court decisions that referenced the hair testing results. I met with young adults who had personally been through the child protection system. I also initiated calls for submissions from members of the public and held roundtables to provide me with information and advice about potential recommendations.

In accordance with the restrictions set out in the Order-in-Council, I did not and do not express any view about the civil or criminal responsibility of any person. This limitation permitted the Review to focus on the core scientific question. What I found in the Review was a failure by the system to recognize and put a stop to the flawed toxicology results produced by the Lab.

The evolution of the Lab's focus — from its intended research work to its transition into forensic work — helps explain how things went so wrong. Dr. Gideon Koren had come to SickKids in 1982 and had founded the Hospital's Motherisk Program originally as a research laboratory meant to advance research in identifying drugs and chemicals that affect newborns. This allowed the Lab to develop approaches for the treatment of newborns, also known as 'neonates'. Beginning in 1989, the Lab published its ability to analyze neonatal hair. At some point, the Lab's work shifted from academic research to offering expert forensic expert opinions. As it turned out, that shift happened long before the period I was reviewing.

A Research Lab Offers Forensic Expert Opinions

In 2017, Rachel Mendleson from the *Toronto Star* and John Chipman from CBC identified a Colorado murder case from 1993 that had rejected the Lab's hair testing methodology. In that criminal case, the then-laboratory manager testified about the Lab's hair testing results that, she said, disclosed significant use of drug. Her evidence was rejected at the Colorado preliminary hearing largely for the same flaws I identified in the Review: reliance on a screening test, lack of standard operating procedures, and not meeting the standards of a forensic laboratory. This case apparently did not come to the attention of courts in Ontario.

Increasingly, child protection agencies in Ontario turned to the Lab to test parent's (mostly mothers') hair samples for drugs or alcohol. By the late 1990s, the Lab held itself out as the leader at the cutting edge of hair testing. By 2001 the Lab was marketing its research tests. Over time, it made more than 150 presentations to its primary customers and sources of income, Children's Aid Societies. As well, it distributed regular newsletters to Children's Aid Societies. The newsletters referred to the Lab as the only "academic" lab to conduct hair analysis and discussed its application in civil and criminal law, including child protection and custody.

Although the Lab's methodology was largely accepted as scientifically reliable in Ontario, it was woefully unreliable for legal purposes. It is important to put the matter in the context of the differences between scientific tests undertaken for research and clinical purposes, and those undertaken for forensic/legal purposes.

Research vs. Clinical vs. Forensic

In reality, the Motherisk Lab was a research lab without any accreditation until January 2011, when it became accredited as a clinical lab, a process that had started in 2008. The Lab has never been accredited as a forensic lab.

While a research lab, the Lab was part of the SickKids Research Institute. However, the Institute did not provide any operational or analytical oversight to research labs. Rather, the research lab's principal investigator develops its procedures and usually publishes methods and findings for the purpose of advancing scientific discussion. While it is important that research results are right, a research lab is academic in nature and not subject to the same rigour as is a clinical or a forensic lab. Research labs are not in the business of treating or diagnosing patients, let alone giving forensic opinions.

This is in contrast both to a clinical lab and a forensic lab, which both do work that directly involves individuals. Both are subject to accreditation by an accrediting body.

A clinical lab that undertakes tests and produces results for diagnosis, treatment, or prevention provides crucial and timely information. Such tests are critically important. The treating physician needs to know as much as possible as soon as possible to initiate appropriate treatment. The entire focus of the clinical test is to help the patient.

In contrast, a forensic test is undertaken not to treat a patient, but to establish a scientific result for legal use. A forensic test is often called medico-legal because it applies science to legal problems. The hair tests under review were intended to be used for a legal purpose, whether in child protection or in criminal investigations.

All but a small number of the thousands of hair tests done by the Lab between 2005 and 2015 were done at the request of and paid for by their primary customers; Ontario Children's Aid Societies, as well as a number of child welfare services from other provinces. Hair tests were done for legal purposes — for child protection.

When a test is done for a legal purpose, a lab is not burdened with the time constraints that are so crucial in a clinical lab. A forensic lab does not undertake a test to diagnose and treat a patient. Instead, since forensic results will be used later for legal purposes, it is important that the time available be taken to ensure that the results are reliable.

An accredited forensic lab must comply with stringent standards, including retention of the sample tested where possible, as well as documentation of what steps were taken and by whom. From collection through testing and storage, the sample is documented to meet forensic requirements. These requirements are important because proper procedures and documentation allow another scientist to review the particulars of the Lab's methodology and to be in a position to offer an opinion on its reliability for forensic purposes. Forensic scientists are also trained in their responsibility to provide objective and independent expert opinions.

In the Motherisk Review, I concluded that the leaders of the Lab had no experience or training in forensic toxicology or forensic interpretation. The Lab's leaders told the Review that they did not see their work as forensic nor understand the obligations of a forensic expert testifying in court. Their experience was limited to academic research and clinical toxicology. In the result, the Lab's methodology was unreliable for the purpose of conducting forensic tests.

As the Review progressed, the Lab's lack of qualification to perform forensic testing became apparent. The Hospital temporarily suspended the non-research work of the Lab in March 2015 and the following month shut that work down on a permanent basis.

What Went Wrong at SickKids

With the help of our scientists, the Review identified a number of errors in the preparation of the sample, in its analysis and in the interpretation given to the results. I refer to only three, one at each step.

At the preparation stage, until 2011, the Lab's staff did not routinely wash hair samples before subjecting them to analysis. International forensic standards require samples to be washed. Washing removes most of the environmental contamination caused by exposure to drug. For example, cocaine is readily transferred from other people and surfaces. If a hair sample is washed in advance, the analysis can more easily identify drug found on the inside part of the hair, which would more likely result from direct ingestion of the drug, as opposed to drug on the surface of the hair, which could result from simple exposure.

Second, the Lab had problems with the analytical step of the hair testing. At least until 2011, it used an Enzyme-Linked Immunosorbent Assay test, known as ELISA, which it bought from a well-known company in the United States. However ELISA was designed for use only as a preliminary screening test. A screening test does no more than separate samples into two categories of either potentially negative or potentially positive results.

A positive result only means that the drug might be present, but not that it is present. The kit itself expressly warned that a follow-up with a more sophisticated and expensive confirmation test was required, both to identify and to quantify the target drug. There was not a forensic lab anywhere else in the world that used ELISA as the Lab did to identify and quantify drug.

Finally, the Lab's interpretation of the results raised concerns over the entire period. In its reports, the Lab purported to quantify the amount of drug in the hair, usually to an illusory but seemingly precise two decimal places. The Lab also developed and relied on what it called "concentration ranges" as purporting to provide the reader with a sliding scale of interpretation of a positive test. The test results were categorized by reference to those concentration ranges on a scale from 'very low' to 'very high'.

However, the concentration ranges were themselves unreliable because they were based on the Lab's flawed analysis and procedures. As well, the concentration ranges did not take into account the important points that two individuals who ingest the same amount of drug will metabolize it at different rates, resulting in different concentrations. As well, the ranges did not take into account other differences such as the fact that dark hair holds more drug than does light hair. Test results would also be affected by the use of hair product and treatments. The concentration ranges did not meet international forensic standards and did not provide reliable information for the user.

The tests for alcohol had different problems. Those tests, called Fatty Acid Ethyl Esters (FAEE), suffered from their own shortcomings that made results unreliable, such as testing deficiencies, misapplication of cut-offs, and testing of non-standard hair lengths. More importantly, the science evolved so that the type of testing initially used by the Lab was eventually considered to be unreliable. From 2011, the Lab improved its process by sending samples above the appropriate cut-off to its reference laboratory in the United States for a different and more reliable method of analysis.

Overarching problems were rooted in the lack of adequate oversight by the Hospital. As a result, the Lab continued to test hair for forensic purposes before it even received clinical accreditation in 2011. Moreover, clinical accreditation related only to the Lab's processes and did not assess the robustness or reliability of the hair tests. Sadly, the bottom line was that the Lab's hair tests were flawed. They should not have been relied upon to make decisions in either child protection or criminal cases.

How Were the Flawed Results used?

Between 2005 and 2015, the Lab tested hair samples representing more than 16,000 individuals, fifty-four percent of which tested positive for drugs or alcohol. The Review determined that the tests could not be relied upon as expert opinions. It did not consider individual cases. Nonetheless, it was clear that the results were frequently accepted as 'fact' evidence by participants in the system and too often used as a measure of a mother's credibility and/or ability to parent. A positive hair test result from the Lab was perceived as "almost incontrovertible" evidence that corrosively affected the whole course of the resolution or disposition.

In my December 2015 report, I recommended a review of the individual cases affected by the results in my 2015 report. Shortly thereafter, Ontario appointed the Honourable Judith Beaman to inquire into the individual cases. Commissioner Beaman released her report in February 2018. In the course of her Commission she prioritized 1,271 cases of which she identified fifty-six cases where flawed results had a "substantial impact" on the outcome and resulted in the breaking apart of families and relationships. In addition to identifying certain cases, Commissioner Beaman also advanced a number of recommendations to strengthen child protection practices and systems.

In 2017, Ontario also moved to introduce legislation to ensure appropriate accreditation of forensic laboratories, which is a promising initiative.

Finally, in light of the use of the Lab by child protection agencies in other provinces, investigative journalists have worked to draw attention to the problem on a national scale.

Where do we go from here?

There is much to be done to improve child protection systems for all communities. While we, as a society, must protect children from danger, we must also work towards providing families with supports to enable children to stay with their families, kin or communities. Children need the love of families and community.

The Review received moving letters from many parents and others affected by the flawed science. I can only begin to imagine the fear, grief, and despair suffered by so many as a result of these flawed hair tests and their consequences. I found particularly moving a meeting arranged for me by the Provincial Advocate. That meeting was with several young adults who had lived through the system. It was not easy to keep wearing my judicial face while listening to them describe the difficulties and challenges they had faced. I admire their resilience and their hope for a means that will allow them to know more about and to explore their own stories and histories. What was clear is that many children, and even young adults, suffer enduring pain at separation and thereafter from lack of contact with a flawed but much-loved and loving parent. I wish I could wave a magic wand to make it all better for those hurt by flawed science in the justice system. I cannot do that but I do honour all those who work with children and the adults they become to provide them with understanding, acceptance and support. I also honour all those who work with mothers and fathers and families of choice to offer them the supports they need.

For the sake of these children and families, we in the legal system must keep our minds constantly open and vigilant. Our task is to ask questions that will identify unreliable opinions and unqualified experts.

To do this, we must all strengthen our scientific literacy and our own common sense. We must question the science and the scientist about the qualifications of both, about the scope of the opinion, about the particulars of the scientific method and about its uncertainties. When a particular cutting-edge science purports to provide definitive answers, we must approach it with healthy skepticism.

We must remember that science is a tool, not a solution.

A lawyer, arbitrator and judge, as well as a political activist and feminist, Hon. Nancy Morrison practiced law and adjudicated in Ontario, Saskatchewan, British Columbia, Yukon, and Northwest Territories. As a judge, she served for nine years on the British Columbia Provincial court and fifteen years on the Supreme Court of British Columbia. Raised in Yorkton, Saskatchewan, she now lives in Vancouver, B.C.

Hon. Nancy Morrison

The Courage of Vicki

THERE WAS A MEAN SHED in a nearby field. Small and old, a sometime pump house, it had a dirt floor, upright rough-hewn slats for walls, some barbed wire, broken pipes. Inside, feed for cattle. An old bathtub was outside, to be filled with water for the cattle. Its only door could not be seen from the grandmother's farm.

It was one of the places he took the child to rape her.

Vicki Waters was eight when her mother died May 15, 1966, in a tragic car accident. Her car had overturned into a water and mud-filled ditch, not far from their home in Richmond, British Columbia.

At the time, Vicki's older brother Cookie was twelve, her younger brother Gordie was six. Within days of their mother's death, Gordie would turn seven, and Vicki, nine.

Their father, Sabick Singh, from a pioneer East Indian farming family in British Columbia, had his own small trucking business. He made arrangements for a babysitter to look after the two younger children before and after school as he travelled in his work. The older brother, Cookie, had already begun living with his paternal widowed grandmother, the powerful and controlling matriarch of the family, on her farm in Chilliwack, B.C.

As summer approached, Vicki and Gordie began to spend time at the grandmother's farm, and for the next two years, they went to school mostly in Richmond, but weekends, summers, and holidays were spent at the farm. They also spent time at the adjoining dairy farm that belonged to their father's sister and her husband, Darshan Kaur Singh, and Joginder Bains.

It was not an arrangement that either Vicki or Gordie liked. They were sometimes referred to as "the orphans" by some members of the extended family. The grandmother's house was not a kind or loving home for the two bereaved children.

They particularly did not like and feared their aunt's husband, Joginder. He was tall, powerful, bad-tempered and controlling. Born and raised in India, with a university degree in the Punjabi language in a religious course, he was regarded by his wife, Darshan, and others as a Giani, a term of respect for a religious person. When his vicious temper was triggered, he was physically abusive to those who failed his commands, including his wife.

Shortly after her mother's death, Vicki recalled being driven from their home to their grandmother's farm by Darshan and Joginder. She did not want to go with them. She thought Joginder was mean. En route to the farm, they stopped at Mission. The adults got out of the car, and she and Gordie got out with the purpose of running away. Her uncle grabbed her by the hair and smacked her. Gordie was terrified. They both got slapped. "Gordie peed his pants."

When they got to the farm in Chilliwack, again the two young children wanted to get away and they ran into the barn to try and hide. Gordie left the barn; Vicki was in the barn by herself. Joginder came to get her, he was angry. She was afraid of him.

He grabbed her, and brushed up against her rear end, then smacked her again and tried to fondle her, telling her it's okay. She knew it was not — it was not like being touched by her parents.

THAT WAS THE BEGINNING of Vicki's nightmare. She and Gordie spent more time at the grandmother's farm, and at her aunt and uncle's, the nearby Bains farm. Sometimes, they stayed overnight at the Bains house. There were three bedrooms in the house, but only one bedroom was used for sleeping. It had two double beds and one cot. The adults would sleep with the children. This is where everyone slept.

Vicki recalled the first occasion when she was stuck in a bed with Joginder. "That's where things begin." He cuddled up to her, spoon fashion, then put her into his groin area where it was obvious that he had an erection. His penis was out and he put her on top of him face to face. She said there was a lot of rubbing. She was nine.

It was after that when he took her to the little shed.

Joginder had picked her up from the grandmother's farm, purportedly to help him with the heifers. There were others present to help, and she told him she did not want to go, but he took her in his car to the shed, parking on the side where the car could not be seen from the grandmother's farm. He began to fill up the old tub with water, while Vicki was inside with the cattle feed.

Then Joginder came into the shed.

Vicki said that he was always pressing against her, always touchy-feely, fondling. Then he would get quiet, and she knew what was coming. He would get her alone, isolated — like this first time in the shed. Whenever she had tried to resist, she got slapped, struck hard. She was afraid and ashamed. "I can smell him. He touches me too much. His hands are in my pants, his finger in my vagina."

Then he got her pants off.

"I can leave my body and see myself. He picks me up and puts me on his penis, facing me. His eyes are rolling. He slides me back and forth. His penis is then in my anus. I bleed."

He left her on the ground, on the dirt floor, crying. He told her to walk home.

When she got back to the grandmother's, Gordie was in the barn, and she told her little brother in language that he could understand. She was too afraid to tell any adults. Joginder had threatened her never to tell anyone of the assaults, that no one would believe her, that she would not be allowed to visit with her father, or see her little brother. She was terrified and believed him.

For the next few days, Vicki was hurting, and bleeding. She tried to put Vaseline on herself. She felt ripped open. She was walking with difficulty, and she continued to hurt and ache for a few more days. She was nine or ten.

THAT FIRST INCIDENT in the old shed has always stayed with her. There were other occasions in the shed, and while she cannot remember exact dates or times, she has vivid memories of the touching, the sexual acts, how she felt, smelling him.

"Auntie, don't go to town and leave me alone with him."

Her aunt was getting ready to go to town, doing her hair. Watching her, Vicki was distressed, because it meant that she would be left at the Bains house with Joginder and their two young children.

"Please don't leave me. Your husband hurts me, touches me. He's doing things to me. He's putting himself at me." When her aunt asked Vicki what she meant, Vicki told her what was happening.

"We don't talk about these things. Look, you're causing trouble. If you cause trouble, your dad won't want to see you. It's a dirty thing." With that, her aunt left Vicki in her home with her husband. She went to town.

Again, "Joginder had his way." Vicki was ten.

A few days later, Vicki was alone with her grandmother and her aunt Darshan at the grandmother's home. She took the opportunity to tell them what Joginder was doing to her. Vicki thought the grandmother's reaction indicated she already knew.

"I don't want to be left alone with him. I don't like him. He's touching me."

Both her aunt and grandmother told her, "Don't talk about this. It's not happening. Don't bring it up. Don't cause trouble."

Vicki estimated that between the ages of ten and thirteen, she was physically and sexually assaulted by her uncle about once a week.

Joginder took her to a corn field on one occasion to sexually assault her. One time he came and signed her out of her school. Sexual intercourse mainly took place at the Bains' home. Other sexual assaults occurred on the grandmother's farm, in the storage garage, in the barn, in the hay chutes and lofts, in the dairy room. Oral sex was forced "a lot of times."

When Vicki was about twelve-and-a-half, she began to menstruate. She told her grandmother and aunt, and after a couple of months, the periods became regular. On being told of the regular periods, the grandmother and aunt immediately took Vicki to the family doctor in Chilliwack. She had seen the doctor before for infection, and the flu. She did not know why she was going to see him on this occasion. Her aunt and grandmother went in to see the doctor, and came out ten minutes later. A nurse came out and told Vicki to come in to the examination room.

She was asked when her last period had occurred, then told to undress, put on a gown and get up on the table. Her feet were placed in stirrups. Something was inserted into her, which caused a terrible pain in her back, and she felt nauseous. She was crying, lying there. She was told to get dressed and went out to the waiting room where her grandmother and aunt were. They said little to her, and drove her back to the grandmother's farm. No comforting, no explanations.

It was not until ten years later that Vicki realized what had been done to her in that doctor's office. Newly married, she and her husband knew something was wrong when the condoms were getting cut during intercourse, and her husband's penis was also being cut. They went to a doctor in Vancouver, and after a scan, it was obvious — Vicki had a deteriorating Copper T7 IUD in her. It had to be surgically removed.

By the time Vicki experienced the IUD insertion, she and Gordie were living full time at the grandmother's farm, attending school in Chilliwack, and doing farm chores for the grandmother and the Bains, including helping with the cows, cleaning out the barn, cutting hay, grass, and spreading manure, with Vicki also helping with meals and the small Bains children.

For ten years, until Vicki graduated from high school and left the farm at the age of eighteen, she was repeatedly raped, sodomized, and forced to perform oral sex, with continual physical abuse and threats by her uncle.

In her teens, one of the few people whom Vicki trusted was a young and dashing uncle of hers whose work took him back and forth from Vancouver to the grandmother's farm. He was kind to her, and had liked Vicki's deceased mother, unlike some of the other members of the family.

When Vicki was fourteen or fifteen, her young uncle began an affair with her. Vicki was desperate to be loved, and was infatuated with him. She told him of Joginder's sexual assaults, but nothing changed.

On graduating from high school, Vicki moved to Chilliwack to live with her older brother for a short time, working as a bookkeeper. She then moved in with Marilyn Dwornick, who became, and remains, her close friend and confidante. Both young women had experienced sexual assaults, and they confided in one another.

In late 1981, Vicki met Rodney Waters, a heavy equipment operator, and they were married in April, 1982 in Las

Vegas. They have two children, a son and a daughter.

The abuse that began in September 1966 ended in 1975 when Vicki turned eighteen and left the farm. In spite of marrying a loving and supportive husband, and being proud of her two children, Vicki's life over the years was marked by self-destructive behaviour, at times drinking too much, experimenting with drugs in her earlier years, sexual promiscuity before her marriage, long bouts of anxiety, depression, and continuing difficulty in trusting people.

There had been marital problems, difficulty with child rearing, with most of that being done by her husband. She has experienced impaired sexual functioning, sleep difficulties, and deep feelings of shame and humiliation.

With the support of her husband, Vicki frequently sought medical and counselling help. In her early and formative years, her education opportunities and obvious intellectual capacity were never recognized or encouraged, and she was never provided the opportunity to learn and appreciate her cultural background.

It took Vicki Waters a long time to come to terms with what had happened to her and to decide to bring the abuse out in the open, and finally, into court, insisting that initials not be used to hide her identity. Almost thirty years after the abuse ended, in 2005, she began a civil action, suing her aunt and uncle in the Supreme Court of British Columbia. The claim against her uncle was based on allegations of sexual assault. Her claim against her aunt was that in spite of disclosures of the sexual assaults at the time to her aunt, the aunt breached her duty of care to her, or alternatively, was liable in negligence by reason of her failure to act to protect Vicki from the harm she was suffering by the actions of her husband, Joginder Bains.

Vicki claimed physical and psychological harm, impairment of a normal and proper childhood, social, interpersonal and sexual development, impairment of her ability to maintain a normal marital and sexual relationship with her husband, and an inability to trust others, or control her emotions.

The case was brought in the Supreme Court of British Columbia and came before me, with nine days of evidence ending September 27, 2007.

The evidence of Vicki, her husband, her friend Marilyn, and younger brother Gordie was compelling. And heartbreaking. There was powerful and uncontested psychiatric evidence from a medical expert who had extensive experience counselling female victims of sexual abuse. He had interviewed Vicki on four separate occasions in preparation of his medical/legal report.

When giving her evidence, Vicki was very emotional at times, and apologized frequently, something that the medical expert had observed in his interviews, the same frequent apologizing. But Vicki Waters was telling the truth, what had happened to her, testifying about memories that still possess her. I had no hesitation in accepting her evidence. It was not embellished, it was given with great difficulty.

The defendants categorically denied each and every claim, with Joginder testifying that Vicki and Gordie were untruthful about everything. When Joginder testified at trial, it was in the manner of an educated and very assertive man. I did not believe him. Where his evidence differed from that of Vicki Waters or her brother Gordie, I accepted the evidence of Vicki and her brother.

Darshan Bains was unable to attend court for medical reasons, suffering from debilitating arthritis. Her evidence came before the Court by way of her Examination for Discovery.

While there had been a complete denial of everything by the uncle, Joginder, that was not quite the case with Vicki's aunt. At her examination for discovery, Darshan refused to name her doctor. When asked if she and her mother had taken Vicki to see her doctor to have an IUD inserted into Vicki, Darshan's answer under oath was, "I'm sorry, I don't remember. I'm very sorry."

I found the episode of the IUD chilling.

There are some cases where credibility may pose a substantial problem for the trier of fact; this was not one of those cases. The evidence of Vicki Waters was corroborated not only by witnesses called on her behalf, but also in part by witnesses for the defence, in the descriptions of the two homes, the two farms, their layouts, the identification of the family doctor and where he practised.

Credibility is the issue in so many of these cases. This was not a case of recovered memory or flashbacks recalled after counselling. These abuses and memories have always been with Vicki. She had told those few people she trusted at the time of some of the abuses, or shortly after.

Joginder Bains' sexual abuse constituted grievous harm to this child, harm that will last her lifetime. She was so young and vulnerable. She was robbed of those years from eight to eighteen and left to struggle with the ensuing consequences.

This aunt and uncle owed a duty of care to Vicki. There was a breach of that, and the evidence confirmed that they failed to exercise the standard of care required. And Vicki suffered damages as a result of their negligence

The aunt, whom Vicki looked up to, failed to prevent or stop the sexual abuse that she had to have known was going on. Instead, she collaborated with the grandmother to have an IUD inserted into a twelve or thirteen-year-old child, at the onset of puberty, without the consent or knowledge of the child. The inference that I drew was that by having the IUD inserted, both the grandmother and the aunt knew that the sexual abuse by Joginder Bains was ongoing, and they wanted to ensure there would be no pregnancy or discovery of the continuing abuse.

Vicki Waters showed determination in bringing this legal action, with the resulting uncomfortable and public exposure, and personal trauma that she experienced. Vicki wanted to obtain justice in her own case, but also to serve as an example to others who might not be as able to go through the agony and uncertainty of a case in open court.

Vicki felt her aunt and uncle should be responsible for their actions and the resulting harm to her. She sought financial compensation, and an end to the anxiety, humiliation, and shame that she had experienced over the last forty years. She believed it was important for her own healing to be able to speak freely about these matters openly for the first time. She also felt it important to speak out for the benefit of others who may be experiencing the same thing.

She showed intelligence and remarkable resolve in coming forth publicly, against considerable odds. Before the trial commenced, a Vancouver newspaper reporter had picked up the claim, and written an article on the case, after phoning Vicki at her home in Nelson, B.C. to confirm the claim. This triggered strong disapproval of Vicki within the Sikh community, much of which still exists to this day.

On October 5, 2007, I gave reasons for judgment in favour of the plaintiff, Vicki Waters. Vicki wept on hearing the judgment, that finally she had been heard and believed.

After the finding of liability, counsel arranged for trial dates to present evidence and submissions on damages. Counsel for Vicki was seeking general damages including aggravated damages of $350,000 and punitive damages of $100,000.

They were relying upon the case of *Yeo v. Carver, (1996), 26 B.C.L.R. (3d) 155(C.A.),* a 1996 case where a young girl who had been sexually assaulted by her stepfather from age seven to fourteen. There had been no sexual intercourse, but other types of sexual assault including digital penetration. A jury awarded $350,000 for general and aggravated damages, plus $250,000 in punitive damages, totaling $600,000.

The British Columbia Court of Appeal reduced those damages to $250,000 for general damages and $50,000 for punitive, totaling $300,000. The other cases cited awarded significantly lower damages, including cases that followed the Yeo case.

By way of contrast, the defence cited the case of *Hill v. Church of Scientology of Toronto, (1995) 2S.C.R. 1130*, an Ontario decision that ended up in the Supreme Court of Canada. It was a defamation case. Hill was a Crown Attorney who brought an action against the church for libel. The case drew a great deal of attention and several interveners. A jury awarded general damages to Mr. Hill of $300,000, plus $500,000 for aggravated damages, and $800,000 for punitive damages, totaling $1,600,000. This was upheld by the Ontario Court of Appeal, as well as the Supreme Court of Canada.

In *Hill*, the Supreme Court of Canada did not interfere with the jury findings or amounts awarded, even though the plaintiff had received several promotions and then an appointment to the bench by the time of the final trial. Cited as a not-so-subtle jab that our society values damage to reputation more than damage to a child from sexual assault? I did feel strongly that the existing legal precedents on damages for sexual assault at that time were unrealistically low.

My judgment for damages was rendered June 25, 2008. I found that both the aunt and uncle played a significant part in the losses suffered by Vicki, and that both were liable for damages, jointly and severally.

Aggravated damages were called for, there being a need to compensate this plaintiff for the outrageous behaviour by both defendants.

I ordered general damages, including aggravated damages in the amount of $325,000. Punitive damages were awarded in the amount of $80,000, plus $10,000 for the cost of future care, mainly with a view to counselling, plus costs.

At the time, to my knowledge, this was the highest award to any plaintiff for sexual assault in a civil action.

The case did not go on to appeal. It took a long time for Vicki to collect, but damages were eventually paid by the defendants.

Vicki Waters is sixty now, still married, with a son who is a successful professional athlete, and a daughter who is a trained social worker, married with two children. Vicki has consented to her story being told. She still is ostracized by many in her South Asian community, but by others, she is recognized for her courage in speaking out, then, and now.

On May 12, 2011, Vicki Waters was one of the recipients honoured at a gala reception where Coast Mental Health acknowledges everyday heroes with their 'Courage to Come Back' Awards. Vicki was a recipient of that Award. She earned it.

It was Vicki's daughter, Kaitlind Waters, who nominated her mother for the award. Kaitlind said,

> My mother is a woman who courageously stood up to her family in the name of justice ... and who has devoted her time, energy and heart and soul to being the voice of others who have suffered from childhood sexual abuse. This subject is not only taboo in her South Asian background, it is a difficult subject for most victims to talk about.

When Vicki spoke at a forum on violence against women in the South Asian community, several Sikh elders tried to stop her. They were unsuccessful. Following her talk, Vicki received a standing ovation. After, many women lined up to speak to her, and share their stories. Kaitlind saw looks of relief on their faces as they talked with her mother.

Sexual violence against women and children occurs worldwide, in every country, in every society, crossing all racial, ethnic, social and economic lines. No matter where the victims may live, or what age, it takes great courage for them to speak out.

We all have our heroes. Vicki is one of mine.

The Honourable Lise Maisonneuve was appointed Chief Justice of the Ontario Court of Justice (OCJ) in 2015. Appointed to the OCJ in 2003, she presided over criminal matters in the Ottawa area for twelve years, rising to the role of Regional Senior Judge, East Region in 2011 and then Associate Chief Judge of the OCJ in 2013. Before joining the judiciary, she was a partner with the Ottawa firm of Carroll, Wallace and Maisonneuve, where she practiced criminal law.

Hon. Lise Maisonneuve

How To Shift a Culture

ON MARCH 8, 2018, International Women's Day, I was attending a meeting of our Court's administrative judges. These are the judges who, among many other tasks, supervise the sittings of the Ontario Court of Justice (OCJ) and the assignment of judicial duties. In effect, they function as my delegates in the courthouses in which they sit.

That morning, as I looked out at the room and listened to comments from the audience, I was reminded of the progress our Court has made in terms of gender parity. Of the forty-eight judges attending, twenty-four were women.

Over the past several years, it has become the OCJ's normal situation to have balanced numbers of women and men being appointed as Judges and Justices of the Peace. As of March 2018, 126 of 298 judges on our Court are women, which works out to approximately forty-two percent of that bench. Over the past year, twenty-seven of the fifty new appointments have been women. The trends are even more pronounced on the OCJ Justice of the Peace bench where 167 of 304 justices of the peace are women. In the most recent group of thirty-eight new justice of the peace appointments, twenty-two are female.

While we accept this diversity as the status quo today, I know full well we can't be smug or wave aside any concerns about the continuing role of women in our Courts — thinking the battle is won and that women are firmly and permanently ensconced as equal members on our benches. It's one thing to introduce a significant culture change, it's quite another to maintain it over the long term. Further, I know that our Court isn't a perfect reflection of the legal world from which we draw our judges. And, in turn, I know the legal world is not a perfect reflection of the diversity in today's Canada.

Back in March 2016, on the cusp of a previous International Women's Day, I addressed the Women in Criminal Law Conference in London, Ontario. The discussion that day focused on the challenges female defence lawyers face in building and maintaining a practice in a field still dominated by men and framed by men's expectations. This conference came hard on the heels of the release of a report prepared for the Criminal Lawyers' Association which clearly demonstrated that, for a variety of reasons, women were leaving the practice of criminal law at higher rates than men. Retention of women in the private practice of criminal law continues to be a live issue, despite strides in other sectors of the criminal justice system, including our Court.

That brings me to the crux of my chapter. I believe that our Court and its progress toward a more diverse bench, in terms of gender and other aspects of diversity, is far from complete. Nevertheless, the strides we have made as an institution provide a solid case study in how to shift a culture and move toward lasting, positive change.

Judges and Justices of the Peace are the lynchpins of our

justice system. We shoulder a profound responsibility to administer the law with fairness and impartiality. Today, it is accepted that diversity on the bench is intimately linked to the provision of equal justice for all in Canadian courts. But it wasn't always that way.

We've all heard the gurus of organizational change theory tell us that three basic elements are needed to effect lasting change. First, people must accept that change is necessary. Second, that process of transition must be premised on a shared vision for the outcome of that change. Third, systems need to be put into place to ensure change can take root and flourish. Simply put, people need to agree to pull in the same direction, and then they need to actually do some real pulling.

So, let me set the stage for the changes that have occurred in our Court.

Fifty years ago, when our Court was a magistrates' court, a lawyer named David Vanek was appointed to the criminal bench. Writing about the progress he witnessed during his nearly twenty years on our Court, beginning with his appointment in 1968, he recalled:

> Automatically I joined a select brotherhood of the judiciary. It was indeed a fraternal organization because not a woman graced the dais at this time or for several years thereafter."[1]

It wasn't until 1979, over ten years after David Vanek joined the bench, that June Bernhard became the first woman to become a judge in the criminal court, serving with Justice Vanek

1 Vanek, David. *Fulfilment: Memoirs of a Criminal Court Judge* (The Osgoode Society for Canadian Legal History: 1999). pp. 216 and 219. When David Vanek joined the bench in 1968, it was before the creation of the Provincial Courts. The two Provincial Courts were formed later in 1968 – and Vanek was a member of the Provincial Court (Criminal Division). On the Provincial Court (Family Division) at that time, there were only four women: Margaret Chambers, Marjorie Hamilton, Mary Catherine Maloney, and Bertha Thompson.

and the 'brotherhood' in Ontario's Provincial Court (Criminal Division). Even in 1979, her appointment was groundbreaking news, meriting newspaper coverage with headlines like "Woman Judge Makes History." In fact, Bernhard recalled that when the Deputy Attorney General phoned to invite her to join the Court, she thought it was a prank call.[2]

All of our progress has been achieved in one generation, just a few decades. Many of the judges sitting today in our Court remember the days when there was no maternity leave for judges, for example. Supreme Court of Canada Justice Rosalie Abella, who began her judicial career on our Court in 1976, presided until the day before giving birth. She stayed home with her baby for two months, still receiving her judicial salary. When she was told there had been a mistake and that there was actually no maternity leave program for judges, she returned that money.[3]

Today, we shake our heads at these stories. So how did our Court so dramatically increase the percentage of women on its benches? How can we continue to attract women to apply to serve on our Court?

We must be vigilant. As I mentioned, it's one thing to introduce change, it's quite another to maintain it.

Many things must work in concert to ensure that our benches reflect our society.

LET ME GET PERSONAL HERE. I was appointed to be the Associate Chief Justice of the OCJ in 2013. At that time, I joined Faith Finnestad as Associate Chief Justice and Annemarie Bonkalo as

2 Batten, Jack. *Judges* (Toronto: Macmillan of Canada, 1986), p. 91. In fact, Batten wrote about that call, "Bernhard never entirely believed she'd be named to the bench, not even when the big call came. . .'I'm the Deputy Attorney General,' the voice on the phone said. 'And I'm the Shah of Iran,' Bernhard answered. She got the appointment anyway. . ."

3 Karen Cohl, Susan Lightstone, George Thomson. "Diversity: Changing the Face of the Court." Ontariocourts.ca. http://www.ontariocourts.ca/ocjhistory/evolution/diversity-changing-the-face-of-the-court/ (accessed April 2, 2018).

Chief Justice. Three women in leadership positions. It was a first for any court in Canada.

At the time, both men and women congratulated me on my appointment. But a few of the men — and none of the women — asked me how it was working with the Chief Justice and the two Associates all being women. I could tell these men were genuinely concerned, or perplexed. I was afraid they might have thought that the three of us together lacked the collective abilities to lead what was then the largest trial court in Canada.

After I'd figured out the subtext to questions like this, I realized I had a responsibility to 'normalize' our situation for those who still found it unusual. So, I didn't let these questions lie. I would enter into discussions with those who were questioning our leadership abilities, and making assumptions. I wanted to ensure that all were aware that I understood precisely what they were saying and that I wasn't buying into the old views and rules. Our Court has changed. End of story.

Simply put, leaders must lead — vocally and unequivocally. I realize that, thanks to my position, I can contribute to changing the conversation. It's important for me, and leaders like me whether they be men or women, to be direct in pointing out old and out-dated ways of thinking about the world of work and the place of women and men in that world. Gender does not restrict our choices. We should talk together about how we want to shape our work world and our places in it, then must do the work to make change happen.

I would argue that the progress in our Court began with strong leadership. In the late 1980s, changes were introduced to the appointments process used to select judges for our Court. A model was introduced by the Ontario government that emphasized and valued transparency, and promoted merit and diversity. This model still exists, now enshrined in the *Courts of Justice Act,* and it features a broad-based committee, the Judicial Appointments Advisory Committee (JAAC) that advertises judicial vacancies, interviews candidates, and forwards a short list to the Attorney General of those who are best qualified. I think it's worth quoting from the *Courts of Justice Act* to see the statutory regime under which JAAC operates. JAAC not only should assess the professional excellence of candidates for the judiciary but also their "community awareness and personal characteristics" and, further, recognizes "the desirability of reflecting the diversity of Ontario society in judicial appointments."[4] The result of the introduction of JAAC — a profound systemic change — has been a steady stream of exceptionally well-qualified applicants to the OCJ.

I'd like to give you a bit more history.

Positive change didn't just happen because of a change in appointments process. People, both women and men, actively pushed for this progress to occur. They made sure that the good intentions of a piece of legislation became reality. Active steps were taken. For example, in 1990, Howard Hampton, the Attorney General of the day, sent out a letter to all women lawyers in the province who had been in practice for more than ten years inviting them apply to the Court. The letter stated that the government's goal was a Court comprised of at least fifty percent women. That approach was previously unheard of — and some of those women who were encouraged to apply because of that letter sit on our Court to this day. As a result of that strategic move, change occurred. The justice system has, as a whole, benefited.

But change doesn't come pain free. Not everyone was pleased with the growing diversity of judicial appointments in the early 1990s and the push for more women to become judges. One significant example: the first chair of JAAC,

4 Section 43(9), *Courts of Justice Act*, R.S.O. 1990, c. C.43

Professor Peter Russell, recalled receiving a call from a male lawyer, upset by the active encouragement of women applicants. According to Russell, the lawyer said: "I want to be a judge but I don't want to wear a skirt."[5]

The leaders of the Court took action. They determined it was time to invest significant time and effort in ensuring that the Court was welcoming of diversity — and systemic changes were made. During the early 1990s, the Court began delivering comprehensive gender awareness and sensitivity training for the judiciary, involving greater numbers of women in delivering such programs.

THESE EDUCATION PROGRAMS accelerated a real shift in the Ontario Court's culture, as the judiciary of the Court began pulling in the same direction, recognizing the value of a broadly representative bench. The more varied the values, experiences and assumptions within a court as a whole, the more the court will be — and will be seen to be — open to the realities of the diverse public that appears before it.

One of our judges, Justice Manjusha Pawagi, recently expressed the value of diversity succinctly — and I can't say it better

> I recognize the value having a different cultural perspective than many of my colleagues. My cultural lens doesn't take away the need to examine carefully, as all judges must, how my personal background and experience can affect the way I see the cases that come before me. The challenge for all of us is to use cultural sensitivity and avoid cultural bias.[6]

History is instructive but the question remains, *How do we*

5 Karen Cohl, Susan Lightstone, George Thomson. "Diversity: Changing the Face of the Court." Ontariocourts.ca. http://www.ontariocourts.ca/ocjhistory/evolution/diversity-changing-the-face-of-the-court/ (accessed April 2, 2018).

6 IBID.

move forward from here? I believe that Justice Pawagi has identified the critical issue for anyone considering the role of women in the criminal justice arena, or for that matter, the world of work generally. We must be aware of our own personal backgrounds and how they influence our careers and the myriad ways we do our work.

THAT BRINGS ME to my own experiences, the trajectory of my legal career and the responsibilities I believe each of us has as individuals to ourselves and our work lives.

I did not have any sort of firm career plan when I was called to the Bar in 1991. I had graduated from the University of Ottawa Faculty of Law and the two things I knew for certain were that I wanted to stay in Ottawa and I wanted to practice criminal law.

I joined a small firm where I had the opportunity to try my hand at every aspect of criminal law as defence counsel. In those days, my goal was very simple — to do my best at whatever role I was in. I remain firmly committed to this approach. I believe it has served me well.

I learned three vital things in those early years: to watch, to listen and to ask questions of those senior to me. I was persistent. I spent many hours in court, just watching various senior lawyers conduct trials. I was not a particularly confident person in those days and it required a real effort on my part, but I would screw up my courage and strike up conversations with experienced counsel, ask questions, and listen to their answers. After a few months, it became easier to do this. I realized that I was consciously developing confidence in my own skill, my own approach and my own way of communicating. I was learning to do things on my terms.

I talked to everybody. I wanted all the members of the Ottawa bar, both men and women, to see that I was part of their group of criminal defence lawyers. I joined the local criminal defence counsel association. I pitched in. As mentioned, I was persistent. I realize now that, to use a phrase Sheryl Sandberg coined, I was "leaning in."

But that wasn't enough. I knew I needed to continue learning. I asked a couple of the lawyers I'd met to mentor me. They were senior lawyers whose approach to both work and life I admired. I made a conscious decision to find both male and female mentors. They gave me important support in the development of my skills as a lawyer and as a person. They encouraged me to develop my own style and voice as a litigator — not simply to replicate their approaches. When my work was critiqued by my mentors, I paid attention to the comments and I took them seriously. I told myself not to take those criticisms personally. Again, like acquiring confidence, it took me time to get to that place where I didn't feel personally deflated and defeated by criticism. I believe my ability to learn from the comments of others made me a stronger advocate for my clients — and able to withstand the rigours of practice.

I UNDERSTAND that the readers of this book will be a varied lot, but I know that many women will read it pondering their futures in the criminal law arena. In this book, you'll read many essays from experienced criminal lawyers — all women — who, despite the many challenges they faced in continuing and succeeding in their careers, persisted. In turn, their contributions to the law have had important and positive impacts for both individuals specifically, and society as a whole. They are examples for us all. In light of those stories, I see one of my roles as Chief Justice as encouraging women to follow in their footsteps. Part of that role involves encouraging and maintaining the gender diversity of our Court today as an administrative function as Chief Justice. But another part of my role is personal — telling my own story and the lessons I have learned and can share.

On a personal level, I'd suggest that anyone interested in doing work similar to those who have contributed to this book look at their personal situations from two complementary perspectives: plan your career strategically, and think long term.

The act of planning strategically — finding mentors, talking with your colleagues, reading books like this one — allows you to imagine how you might react in various challenging circumstances and will make you more flexible when the future unfolds and you need to make personal and career choices.

Then, there's thinking long term. I know many of the judges on our Court knew early on in their legal careers that they would one day apply for the bench, and so they made a point of speaking to judges and others about the steps they should be taking — for example, the sorts of activities and volunteer work in which they should participate. And, they went about building their resume. As many will tell you, a legal career will never unfold precisely as imagined. Nevertheless, you'll be prepared for what does occur if you plan for the long run — and have considered the potential bumps in the road.

Being strategic means objectively assessing your strengths and weaknesses, thinking about the work-life balance that suits you. That objectivity will often come from listening to your mentors' assessment of your abilities, both strengths and weaknesses. Being strategic will mean that you are not making rash decisions you might make without a plan in place.

To those readers of this book who have years of experience in the legal world, both men and women — consider offering a hand to those coming behind you. It serves no purpose to tell tales of how hard you had it, without committing to improving the lot of those who will be practising long after you've retired. Encouraging and supporting newcomers will only make the entire legal system better, fairer and more accessible to all. And isn't that what we want?

As my walk through a slice of the OCJ's history demonstrates, cultures and organizations change. Our Court has changed dramatically over the past few decades with the inclusion of women on our benches. Those changes will continue. The justice system and the legal profession have learned, and are continuing to learn, that diversity pays many dividends. Social fairness is just one.

Hearkening back to my earlier comments, for change to continue, people need to get behind those changes and keep pushing. Active steps must be taken, both individually and collectively. Change becomes reality when people come together, talk about ideas and, then, transform those ideas into reality.

After obtaining her law degree at Sherbrooke University Faculty of Law, Danielle Côté was admitted to the Bar in 1978. Appointed judge of the Court of Québec in 1994, she is now Associate Chief Judge for the criminal and penal division of the Court of Québec. She has been on faculty at Sherbrooke University, Université du Québec à Montréal, and at Ecole de formation professionnelle du Barreau du Québec.

Hon. Danielle Côté

Certainty? Certainly Not.

DEVASTATED. How could I possibly have felt otherwise? Upon hearing her client's name at the call of the roll, a defence lawyer told me in theatrical tones that her client had taken his own life after I'd found him guilty of the indecent assault of his adopted son.

I will forever remember that morning. The courtroom was full because it was a docket court. The clerk called the accused's name and his lawyer stood up, looked at the people in the court and said to me

> Your Ladyship, you will remember that this is the case where you found my client guilty of indecent assault After the trial, well, I have to tell you that he committed suicide two days later.

Silence echoed in the packed courtroom. Everyone turned

to look at me — the clerk, lawyers, accused, witnesses, police officers, everyone there. I was speechless and frozen with anger for the lawyer who could have had the kindness of giving me the information before that day. She could have simply said that her client had died, without all the theatrics.

I suppose she may have still been convinced of her client's innocence, but this, to me, was not sufficient to justify such conduct. I wondered, *Was she suggesting that I was responsible for her client's suicide?* What a statement full of blame, and how harsh! *Should I be expected to bear the burden of this unfortunate suicide? How can a lawyer address the Court as if she was certain of the innocence of her client?* Certainty is a concept that even science refuses to refer to, since there are few things that could be referred to as certain.

To add insult to injury, the lawyer who uttered the distressing comment is one of the best of the criminal defence bar, one whom I highly respect — a lawyer who makes my day a great day when she is in front of me because she is so capable. She gets right to the point and is brilliant. I know that she respects me, so why would she do such a thing?

As much as I wanted to tell her what I thought of her comment at that moment, I just could not open my mouth because all I was thinking was, *Did he truly kill himself because I erred and he was innocent and his death is the result of a wrongful conviction? Or did he kill himself because he was remorseful? Or maybe because he was suffering a serious depression?* We will never know.

I had asked for a pre-sentence report and in the report, the accused maintained his innocence, but this had not affected my thinking. People sometimes maintain innocence in spite of evidence to the contrary, particularly in sexual assault cases. The night before the lawyer's distressing comment, I had read the pre-sentence report and my judgment, and I was well-prepared to hear submissions on sentence.

This happened fifteen years ago now but my memory of

that moment is as vivid as ever. Not only the visual memory of the moment but the feelings I had — how tortured I was and how many nights I lay awake wondering if I was the cause of this desperate act.

I reread my judgment many times and thought that I had sound reasons to disbelieve the accused and give credit to the complainant's version, yet, this situation was haunting me.

Unreasonable Doubt

Over subsequent months when I would preside over sexual assault trials, I would continually ask myself if I was doing it the right way. I even thought at one point about asking the administrative judge to give me other cases, that I could not do a sexual assault trial again.

Finally, I realized that I would find no solace if I did not take the time to listen to the audio tapes made at the trial, which had been held on two different days. So I did it.

This was a historical sexual assault case (at the time of the crime, it was still labeled indecent assault): the complainant testified about events that had happened twenty years before. At the time of the trial, I had been a judge for ten years and this type of case was, for me, among the most difficult to judge.

Assessing the credibility of a witness, as opposed to reliability, is often difficult. Even more difficult is assessing the credibility of an adult testifying about an assault that occurred when he was a child. It is never an easy task.

So there I was — my weekend dedicated to listening to the audiotape of the trial.

The complainant testified that he was a boy of only eight years old when the events started and the accused was fifty-one. As previously mentioned, the accused was his adoptive father.

According to the boy's version, at the time of the offences

he was often alone with his adoptive father, the accused, who was unemployed. The boy's mother worked full time.

The accused would invite him into his room, where they would undress. The accused would perform oral sex and, afterwards, ask the boy to do the same. When the accused ejaculated, the boy said he would go to the toilet to regurgitate.

The boy also remembered that the accused tried to sodomize him but stopped when he told him how much it hurt. However, the accused would use the threat of sodomy later in their relationship, menacing to try it again if the boy did not act according to his will.

The accused would show the boy pornographic magazines to arouse him — he particularly remembered one where there was 1001 different positions to have sexual relations.

In cross examination, when asked why he decided to lay a charge so many years after the events, the complainant, now in his twenties gave an explanation. He told the Court that he learned that the accused had had two daughters. The complainant talked to the accused's new spouse and told her his story because he did not want the daughters to be assaulted in the same way he was. She did not believe him. He went to the police.

Mind at Rest

In his statement to the police, the accused had denied the allegations and gave many excuses refuting the complainant's version of the events. Testifying for his defence in court, the accused did not really deny the allegations — instead he insisted that he had nothing to be ashamed of because he had polled other people as to whether they believed that he could behave in such a way. At trial, his cross examination by the Crown attorney as regards this statement was a textbook on how to challenge a witness's credibility.

After listening to the audiotapes of the courtroom

proceedings, I finally felt at ease with my judgment. One last time, I read my written judgment and I was convinced all over again beyond a reasonable doubt that the man was guilty.

After I had put my mind to rest, I asked myself why I had to undergo such a gruelling exercise to regain my peace of mind. I had been a judge for many years and I knew that I had never delivered a verdict or passed sentence without being sure that I had done so with the best of my knowledge and belief, and in good conscience.

I suppose I needed to listen to the tapes of the trial because no judge wants to wrongfully convict an accused. The other reason was that learning about the suicide was so shocking that it had traumatized me.

Speaking for myself, historical sexual assault and sexual assault cases are the most difficult cases to try as judge alone without a jury. You do not want to convict an innocent person, but sometimes you also want to convey to the complainants that even if you acquit, this does not necessarily mean that they are not believable.

I am reminded of another case. At a Christmas party at a medical clinic the complainant asserted that the accused touched her breasts two or three times during the dinner. There were twelve witnesses, all of them credible but, because of the circumstances, their reliability was difficult to assess. The accused did not testify. I acquitted.

I did the same thing I had been doing since being appointed — I justified that this was a case where I had to acquit the accused because the Crown's evidence did not convince me beyond a reasonable doubt, even though the complainant was believable. This is the way I explained it in my reasons:

> As pointed out by the defence lawyer, if the Crown's evidence would rely only on the complainant's evidence, the accused would have had to testify to refute

> the allegations. But this is not the case. If this case would have been a civil matter, this Court would conclude to the accused's liability because in civil matters the burden of proof is the balance of probabilities and in this Court opinion it is more probable than not that the accused did what is alleged against him. But in criminal matters the burden of proof is higher and the evidence must convince the Court beyond a reasonable doubt, the Crown did not discharge this burden, thus you are acquitted.

The accused was the Coroner in Chief of the Province of Quebec at the time of the verdict, so his case was a high-profile one. The evening news that night started out with the headline 'Aquitted but Guilty."

The same phrase was repeated in the morning papers the day after and an uproar arose on radio hotlines. A week later the accused filed a complaint against me to the Quebec Judicial Council, arguing that I had breached sections 1, 2, 4 and 5 of the *Code of Ethics for Judges*, which reads

> The judge should render justice within the framework of the law;
>
> The judge should perform the duties of his office with integrity, dignity and honour;
>
> The judge should avoid any conflict of interest and refrain from placing himself in a position where he cannot faithfully carry out is functions;
>
> The judge should be, and be seen to be, impartial and objective.

Obviously the complaint was written by the accused's lawyer and I found it greatly disturbing. In a nutshell it asserted that because of my reference to the civil burden of proof, he then had been found guilty by the public and the media.

Awaiting the decision of the Judicial Council, I resolved to never again refer to the civil burden of proof when acquitting an accused in a case where I believed the complainant.

Three months later I received the decision. I had been right and there were actually appeal court decisions condoning my attitude. What a relief! I had not been responsible for a media frenzy and had not breached my code of ethics.

Lessons Learned

I wanted to share these experiences because I think that more often than not, people do not realize how difficult the act of judging is.

I remember when I was a Crown attorney pleading a difficult sentence there were often sound arguments coming from both Crown and defence, jurisprudence going both ways. I would not give a range to the judge, telling myself that he was well paid to make the call.

Once appointed, I realized that I am now the one making the call. I confess that it is much more difficult than I had anticipated. Of course, there are easier cases than the ones I have just recalled, where the decision is more obvious. But there are those where you live with the case for many days, and sometimes, as in my situation, for many years.

At the end of the day, what lessons do I retain from these experiences?

Lesson one is that a judge is a human being, not immune to making mistakes. A judge does not want to make a mistake, after all we are supposed to know the law and be gifted with a solid reasoning that should prevent us from committing mistakes. But the truth is, even the best judge with the greatest abilities can make an error. And as a judge, I am always alone with the burden of my decision, and only have myself to blame if an error is made.

A judge is ultimately alone when deciding a case and is

always alert to the danger of a wrongful conviction. The truth is that not only is the judge alone, but if a wrongful verdict is rendered, also keenly aware that many may point out the judge as being a bad judge, incapable of rendering justice.

Perfection is not possible. It is out of reach for human beings. A good judge is always trying to reach perfection. But is there certainty? Certainly not. But reaching for perfection helps me sleep at night.

I have been a judge for twenty-four years and there is not one day where I do not tell myself how privileged I am. I love being a judge and love having the feeling that, on most days, I am making a difference in people's lives.

Called to the bar in 1991, Iona Jaffe spent the next twenty-five years as a criminal prosecutor with the Public Prosecution Service of Canada (formerly the Department of Justice). For the last fifteen years of her employment with the PPSC, Iona was a member of the Anti-Organized Crime Team, prosecuting primarily large-scale drug cases and national security matters. In 2017, Iona was appointed to the Ontario Court of Justice and now presides in Brampton, Ontario.

Hon. Iona Jaffe

The Toronto 18

IT WAS JUST A REGULAR WORK DAY in May 2006 when my boss at the Public Prosecution Service of Canada called me into his office. I was in my fourteenth year as a career prosecutor, most of which I spent prosecuting drug offences of one kind or another. I sat across the desk from him unsure of why he had summoned me. "Would you agree to join a team set to prosecute members of a terrorist group?" he asked. A lead counsel had already been selected and he was in the process of selecting a team of other prosecutors to join him. With some hesitation, I agreed.

The idea intrigued me, but I had absolutely no experience in terrorism prosecutions. I was not alone. No one in my office of over a hundred prosecutors had any experience prosecuting terrorism offences. Since the anti-terrorism provisions of *The Criminal Code* were enacted in the wake of September 11, 2001, there had only been one other terrorism prosecution in

Canada, that of Momin Khawaja, which was ongoing in Ottawa at the time.

During the meeting with my boss, all I was told about the case was that it involved a group of individuals planning a terrorist attack. I had no other details. But even with those scant details, I was sworn to secrecy. Until arrests were made, no one but the other members of the prosecution team could know that I was on the case.

I went back to my office and sat at my desk, unsure of what I had just agreed to. A colleague walked into my office and sat down. I knew he had involvement in providing legal advice to the national security investigators working on this case. I felt I could confide in him that I had been assigned to the case but admitted that all I knew about it was that it involved the planning of a terrorist attack. I asked him if he knew where the attack was to take place.

Bound by his own sense of confidentiality, he did not reveal any details. But he did make a gesture with one hand. He pointed down to the ground. I was clearly confused. He pointed to the ground again. It was at that moment, sitting in my office on the 35th floor of the Exchange Tower in Toronto, that it struck me. My colleague was pointing to the floor of the Exchange Tower. "This building is the target of the terrorist attack?" He just looked at me, and I knew I was right.

To say I felt an instant sense of unease was an understatement. I wanted to leave the building of course, but my feelings of anxiety were mixed with feelings of guilt. I had knowledge and could leave the building if I wanted. But I could not share what I knew with anyone else in the building. Not yet. And I could not tell my family that the building to which I commuted everyday was apparently in the cross-hairs of a terrorist group.

SHORTLY AFTER BEING ASSIGNED to the case, I attended a meeting at a police detachment. Police officers, representatives from other agencies, the prosecutors and a paralegal attended the meeting. The room was packed. I had been told in advance of the meeting that I would be in charge of disclosure, meaning I would assist the police in reviewing, organizing, editing, and disclosing what was anticipated to be thousands of pages of notes and documents and multiple terabytes of electronic data. I had been involved in organizing disclosure on cases before, but nothing close to this scale and never on a terrorism file. While I tried to project confidence in my abilities to tackle this responsibility, I felt overwhelmed by the task that lay ahead.

In the days that followed, I began to learn some details. Investigators had been focusing on the activities of a group of young men in Mississauga and Toronto who had organized (and attended) a training camp in Orillia. This was not your run-of-the-mill winter camping trip — young men bonding over ice fishing and bonfires. Far from it.

A quiet patch of cottage country woods was, for a week, transformed into a base-camp for terrorist military training and indoctrination. The men, decked out in full camouflage with faces covered, participated in a series of combat exercises, complete with firearms. Loudly chanting *jihadi nasheeds*, the men marched through the woods in single file, 'stormed' up small hills and victoriously planted on the snowy hillside, a black flag — the kind that has become a certain identifier for most Islamic terrorist groups.

The post-production training camp video was set to music and to the sound effects of explosions. Designed to impress and recruit, the final product had the chilling hallmarks of an Al Qaeda propaganda video.

In the wake of the training camp, the two co-directors, Fahim Ahmad and Zakaria Amara, separated, each pursuing their own terrorist goals. Fahim Ahmad was continuing to organize training camps. Zakaria Amara, and his senior executive Shareef Abdelhaleem had bigger plans.

By the time I was assigned to the case in May 2006, Zakaria Amara's plans were well underway. He had recruited two university students who would assist him in acquiring the necessary equipment. He had manufactured, and tested a remote-control detonator, and his friend Shareef Abdelhaleem put him in touch with someone who could acquire large quantities of ammonium nitrate. Buying in bulk appealed to Zakaria and saved him the trouble of purchasing smaller quantities from various garden centres, a plan which Zakaria had already researched. If all went as planned, in just a few months, Zakaria Amara would orchestrate the detonation of three one-tonne ammonium nitrate bombs at three locations —The Exchange Tower and CSIS building in downtown Toronto, and a military base.

But things were not going to go as planned for Zakaria, because unbeknownst to him, the person through whom he had purchased three tonnes of ammonium nitrate, was not working for him. Zakaria's connection was in reality working for the RCMP. Every conversation the police agent had with Zakaria and Shareef was being recorded, and every instructional note given to the agent by the bomb plotters, was quickly passed on to the police.

The 'ammonium nitrate' was to be delivered on June 2nd, and police planned to make the arrests immediately after the delivery. Rest assured, we were told, there would be no risk to the public. The ammonium nitrate was fake. Investigators were monitoring the movements and conversations of the terrorist group members. The threat was contained.

Despite these assurances, as the take-down day approached, waves of unease washed over me. I was unable to sleep, and I was consumed with a kind of worry that I found difficult to articulate. Even if I could articulate it, I was bound by secrecy and could not share my worries with anyone outside the circle of investigators and prosecutors involved in the case. *What if Zakaria Amara had contingency plans? What if the police did not know everything the group had planned? What if terrorist associates reacted violently to the arrests?* As the take-down day drew nearer, my concerns grew.

On Friday, June 2, 2006, Saad Gaya and Saad Khalid began the laborious task of unloading a large number of white 'ammonium nitrate' bags from a truck. The two men appeared to be enjoying themselves, laughing and chatting as they methodically stacked the bags inside their rented warehouse. Their fun came to an abrupt end as a team of heavily armed tactical officers arrived on scene and arrested both men at gun point. By the end of the day, fifteen other men would be arrested. The arrest of another man weeks later would bring the total number arrested to 18, and forever brand the group, "The Toronto 18."

June 6, 2006 was a day unlike any other at the Brampton courthouse. On the roof of the six-floor building, police snipers were positioned at every corner. Helicopters hovered above a jammed parking lot. Journalists from a multitude of domestic and foreign news agencies swarmed the entrance to the courthouse. And the line-up to enter the courthouse was seemingly endless. The line barely moved, as each member of the public was wanded and their personal possessions x-rayed.

A colleague and I slowly made our way into the courthouse. It all seemed so surreal and the attention being given to these arrests only added to the unease I had been experiencing. We finally arrived at the courtroom and after convincing the guards at the door that we were on the prosecution team, we set up in a small anteroom while the group of arrested men made their first court appearance.

Following the arrests, I was immediately plunged into the virtual ocean of material which this year-long multi-agency investigation had generated. Over seventy-thousand intercepted communications, the notes of hundreds of investigators, 1,500 exhibits seized from various locations, and ninety hard drives containing almost five terabytes of data. Myself, a paralegal, and several other prosecutors, read, edited, electronically scanned and organized the material, so that the first wave of disclosure was given to the defendants six weeks after their arrests. Several more waves of disclosure followed in the ensuing months. We sat for months in a windowless room in the bowels of a police detachment, surrounded by yellow highlighters and Post-it notes, painstakingly reading through stacks of binders.

While this process was underway, bail hearings and pre-trials were being held and the case began to take shape. It would be about a year before we emerged from the disclosure process to dive head-first into the next phase — preparing for trial.

One of my first responsibilities was to listen to hundreds of communications which had been intercepted between the group members in the months leading up to their arrests. The conversations ranged from the banal — such as the December phone call in which Fahim complained to his girlfriend that she had not packed the cans of tuna for the winter camping trip, as he had asked her to do, to the frightening — such as the February conversation caught on the car probe in which Zakaria was overheard enthusiastically telling Fahim that he had just built his first "radio frequency remote control detonator." In that February conversation, Zakaria qualified his success by explaining that the detonator only works from "thirty feet away," to which Fahim replied "thirty feet away? So you have to get blown up? Might as well sit in the car." Zakaria assured him it was "a step forward", and they both agreed that once it works at three-hundred feet, they would "do it."

Another one of my tasks was to view hundreds of jihadist propaganda videos which numerous of the accused had stored on their hard drives, and which Zakaria and Fahim had used to recruit new members. Many of the videos contained graphic footage of terrorist attacks and their gruesome aftermaths. I watched literally hundreds of hours of this type of footage, and we selected a relatively small subset of these videos to tender into evidence at trial. At the conclusion of an admissibility motion, our experienced judge ruled that some of the videos could not be used in evidence because their probative value was outweighed by their prejudicial impact. In other words, admitting them into evidence could undermine the fairness of the trial. There were however, some videos that were admitted but only if the Crown edited the videos to remove scenes of executions and burned bodies, and other "close up or graphic depictions of the dead."[1]

AND SO IT WAS that weeks later, I found myself in court, arguing with defence counsel about whether the scenes that remained in the edited videos depicted a dead person (which would require further editing), or just a severely injured person (which did not need to be edited). I know that for myself and defence counsel, that motion was both surreal and poignant. While the Court and counsel remained sensitive to the subject matter, I could not help but be saddened by how the most tragic events in a family's life, forever captured on video, were being discussed in a Brampton courtroom, like any other item of evidence. I began to realize the many days I had spent watching the videos had clearly started to desensitize me to their graphic content. No longer did I need to cover my eyes as much, or turn my head as quickly. Instead, I would zoom in to the footage, to determine whether I had sufficiently complied with Court's editing order. This particular motion brought back into sharp focus the human toll depicted in the videos which, sadly, is what makes them such effective recruiting tools.

There would be dozens of court appearances over the years. With each one, the frenzy that accompanied the arrests diminished a little, and so too did my anxiety. There was no retaliation from the group, no unexpected detonation of a

1 *R. v. Ahmed,* [2009] O.J. No. 6154 (S.C.J.), at para. 114.

hidden bomb, not even an unkind word expressed by any of the arrested men. It turned out that a significant challenge which confronted me had nothing to do with a physical threat from a terrorist group. The challenge was to stay focused on a case which, from the start, seemed to be the target of media cynicism and public suspicion. Each day brought news reports which appeared specifically designed to undermine the public's confidence in the case.

The Crown's decision to stay charges against peripheral members of the group — a decision commonly made by prosecutors in an effort to streamline and focus a prosecution — was reported as a "setback." It was reported that "the Crown's case was unravelling." Of course I knew the case was not unravelling, but it would have been inappropriate for the Crown to have publicly expressed confidence in its case.

In one newspaper article which appeared the day after the Crown stayed charges, the reporter asked sarcastically if the Crown would "have anyone left it wants to try."[2] It did. Ten adults and one youth. By the end, all eleven men would be convicted of terrorism charges. Two were convicted by juries, two by a judge alone, and the remaining seven — including the terrorist group leaders, and three of the four bomb plot members — admitted guilt.

Zakaria Amara and Fahim Ahmad admitted that for twelve days at the end of December 2005, they co-hosted a camp the purpose of which was to provide training to potential recruits and assess their suitability for their terrorist group. They admitted that the goal of their group was to carry out various acts of terrorism.

They also admitted that they had contemplated purchasing a piece of property in the town of Opasatika, a ten-hour drive north of Toronto. The property was to be used as a possible

2 Thomas Walkom, *Toronto Star*, April 16, 2008

safehouse and training site for their terrorist group. Zakaria admitted what police had already observed several times: that in March and April of that year, he would use a computer in a Meadowvale library to research such topics as ammonium nitrate, rocket fuel, fuel tablets, explosives, and fertilizer.

By the end of March 2006, Zakaria and Fahim had parted ways. Zakaria had effectively broken up with Fahim, out of concern that Fahim was taking too many risks. He expressed his frustration after learning that Fahim had sent a video clip from the training camp to associates overseas. Their foreign connections were apparently impressed with the clip, but Zakaria remained concerned that their faces were visible.

Zakaria admitted that from then on, he and a small group of trusted associates were taking steps to detonate three bombs. In April, Zakaria's friend Shareef Abelhaleem introduced him to someone who purportedly had connections to a chemical company. Zakaria admitted placing an order for one-and-a-half tonnes of ammonium nitrate and some nitric acid. This new associate was in fact, a paid police agent, and Amara's handwritten order had been promptly turned over to the police. By the end of May, Amara increased his order to three tonnes of ammonium nitrate — one tonne for each of the three bombs.

Also, by the end of May, Zakaria had given the police agent a computer memory stick, which had, by then, become Zakaria's preferred method of communicating with the bomb-plot members. Saved on the memory stick was a video in which Zakaria demonstrated the remote control detonator he had constructed. The demonstration showed that a simple call to a cell phone could trigger the explosion. In the videotaped demonstration, Zakaria caused sparks to travel across his living room floor and ignite a toaster. Zakaria was not alone in the room during the demonstration. The footage shockingly captured a glimpse of Zakaria's young child, lying on his stomach with head propped up in his hands as toddlers tend to do, watching with interest. As the police would soon find out when they covertly searched

Zakaria's apartment, the exploded toaster left a burn hole in his carpet. To be sure, the real thing was intended to leave a much bigger mark.

Zakaria was not the only one who videotaped a demonstration. The RCMP videotaped a demonstration of their own. In September 2008, on a flat, remote expanse of land in Alberta, the RCMP Explosives Disposal Unit set out to demonstrate the potential blast effects of a bomb produced according to Zakaria's recipe of one tonne of ammonium nitrate mixed with diesel fuel. I admit I was against the demonstration. I doubted that the effects of the bomb could be effectively demonstrated in such a controlled setting. There were real life explosions, such as the Oklahoma City bombing, which I felt could better capture the potential destruction of Zakaria's plans. Lead counsel was of a different view, and so it was that the RCMP got the green light to proceed. What resulted was a chilling video which, despite my misgivings, clearly conveyed the destructive force of the intended bomb. The explosion severely damaged a two-tonne steel shipping container which was sitting twenty metres from the bomb and caused it to tumble across the field like a weightless tin can. This experiment convinced Crown experts that the blast of such a bomb would have caused catastrophic damage to nearby buildings, and without a doubt, would have injured or killed everyone in its path.

Right from the start, I had been aware that two police agents played important roles in the investigation and that they would be important witnesses in the prosecutions. These two men were very different. Mubin Shaikh, who attended the winter training camp, was outgoing, extroverted, and parlayed his involvement in the investigation into a successful career as a national security consultant.

Shaher Elsohemy, the one who held himself out as a contact through whom Zakaria could acquire bomb-making chemicals, was low-key and private. He had been a friend of Shareef Abelhaleem and it was through Shareef that he was introduced to Zakaria. Far from seeking a spotlight, immediately after he testified, the second agent disappeared and assumed a new life.

I REMEMBER WITH CLARITY a defining moment during one of our preparation meetings with Mr. Elsohemy. We had met as we always did, tucked away in a hotel meeting room at a secret location. It was perhaps my second time meeting the agent, and I confess I was still uncomfortable. After all, he had been friends with Shareef Abdelhaleem, who we were alleging had planned to cause unprecedented harm to the citizens of Toronto. Could I really trust him? The big green elephant in the room of course, was the money he had been paid. *Maclean's* magazine dubbed him "the Mountie's $4-Million Man",[3] though the truth was that he was paid 'up to' $3.9 million, with specific amounts allocated towards various expenses required to set up his new life.

At some point, we needed to confront the agent with the suggestion that a hefty financial gain had motivated him to assist the police. I told the agent that defence counsel would challenge him on his motives, and argue that his credibility had been undermined by a multi-million dollar pay-out. I recall how the agent looked at me as though he was genuinely confused, and even offended by this suggestion. He then pointed out something that had eluded me up until then. Without any mention of a financial reward, he had given the authorities sufficient details to stop the bomb plot in its tracks and make arrests. If I ever had a doubt about whether this agent had legitimately saved Toronto from a terrorist attack, it was gone in that one moment.

It turns out that the topic of money only came up when the police asked the agent if he would work for them, adding, "Oh, by the way, if you do, it will ruin your life." By this they meant that the agent would have to enter the witness protection

3 Michael Friscolanti, *Maclean's*, January 28, 2010.

program, up-root his life and the lives of his immediate family members, relocate, and establish a new reality. Only then did financial negotiations begin. And this raises the question, *How much is someone's life worth?* Not only the agent's life, but the lives he quite possibly saved.

During that same meeting we let Mr. Elsohemy know for the first time that conversations he had with Zakaria Amara and Shareef Abdelhaleem during the investigation had been recorded through a room probe that the police had surreptitiously installed at the gas station where Zakaria worked. The agent was shocked. "You have recordings of our conversations?!" he asked. I admit I was a little concerned. I was thinking, *Is the agent worried that we had recordings of their conversations? And if so, why is he so concerned?* "Yes" we replied somewhat nervously, "We have all of your conversations on tape." The agent let out a huge sigh of relief and exclaimed "I thought you just had my word!!" He could not have been happier to know that there was recorded corroboration of his many debriefings with the investigators.

The agent's indignation at the mere suggestion that he was motivated by money, and his relief at finding out he had been recorded, were spontaneous reactions I wish we could have saved for the courtroom. It would however, be another two years before he walked into court — in January 2010, he came face-to-face with his old friend Shareef Abdelhaleem. By then, three of the four bomb plotters had already pled guilty and only Shareef opted to have a trial. The agent testified over the course of several days, his motives and credibility challenged as predicted. However in the end, the agent's credibility came through. In rejecting the argument that Shareef Abelhaleem had been entrapped by the agent, Mr. Justice Fletcher Dawson found the agent to be a "credible witness".[4] And in a *Maclean's* article titled "A Rat Vindicated",

4 *R. v. Abdelhaleem,* [2010] O.J. No. 5693 (S.D.J.), at para. 61.

Michael Friscolanti wrote that "Today, the truth could not be clearer. Elsohemy was not motivated by dollar bills, and the terrorist plot he helped unravel was very, very real." [5]

Looking back on those early months, I realize now that the negative press and public sentiment were not expressions of distrust in the Canadian justice system. They were more likely expressions of disbelief that a group of young men, who were apparently living peaceful lives in a society which offered them abundant support and opportunity, would be actively planning to destroy that very society. The minimizing and skepticism which had previously infused, if not headlined, many news reports and conversations slowly started to give way to an acceptance that maybe, there was something to this case after all.

I felt a palpable change in media perception and public opinion over time. The day after the youth was convicted after trial, one reporter expressed what others must have started to realize — "There really were Canadian boys and men actively plotting to do damage on Canadian soil…" [6]

It became clear with every guilty verdict or admission by the accused, that the winter gathering in cottage country was not a "hapless adventure in the rain"[7] or a "fat camp",[8] but a terrorist training camp. That the Crown's case was not "bogus",[9] but based on a genuine threat. That the once-described "near-comical portrait",[10] was not so funny after all. And that this 'so-called' terrorist group, was so-called for good reason.

5 Michael Friscolanti. *Maclean's*, January 28, 2010.
6 Christie Blatchford. *The Globe and Mail*, September 26, 2008.
7 Thomas Walkom. *Toronto Star*, April 16, 2008.
8 Isabel Teotonio. *Toronto Star*, April 19, 2008.
9 Thomas Walkom . *Toronto Star*, April 16, 2008
10 Isabel Teotonio. *Toronto Star*, April 15, 2008.

Senator Kim Pate was formerly the executive director of the Canadian Association of Elizabeth Fry Societies. In 2014, she was named a Member of the Order of Canada for advocating on behalf of women who are marginalized, victimized, criminalized or institutionalized, and for her research on women in the criminal justice system. She was appointed to the Senate of Canada on November 10, 2016. She is a member of the Independent Senators Group.

Senator Kim Pate

The Story of S

A Study in Discrimination and Inequality

A FEW WEEKS after I was appointed to the Senate, Lisa Neve called me, as she has nearly every day for the last twenty-five years, asking me how 'senatoring' was going. Lisa is one of my dearest friends and an amazing Indigenous woman. She also urged me to do everything I can to free our friend S.[1]

S, also an Indigenous woman, is currently the longest-serving woman prisoner in Canada. S and I are the same age, but our opportunities and consequent life circumstances are not at all the same. After more than a decade of horrendous physical, sexual and psychological abuse in residential school, she was rendered easy prey for a number of abusive men. Initially jailed as an accomplice to her abusive partner's drug trafficking, in prison she accumulated many more convictions and has spent

1 Although I want everyone to know the injustices that this amazing woman has survived, and I want her exonerated, I am honouring her request to not be identified at this time. Although there are many who support her, she is still in prison and she has every reason to fear reprisal.

most of the past three decades in segregation in many different prisons, in torturous isolation that contributed to her now disabling mental health issues. By all accounts, when S first entered the prison system, she was a nervous, shy, and intimidated young woman.

On March 31, 1993, testifying before the Royal Commission on Aboriginal Peoples (RCAP), S described how, when she was young, she and her mother and siblings would flee her father, sometimes hiding for extended periods in the bush, as he roamed the reservation, sometimes on horseback, shotgun in hand, threatening to kill them all.

Family alcohol and drug abuse encompasses a large part of S's history—a part of her history that is responsible for some of the most traumatic events in her life, including the death of her two brothers: one who overdosed, and one shot to death by a third brother, who was intoxicated. Her father's alcoholism was partially responsible for her falling behind in school. A list of S's family members indicates that almost all are current or past alcohol or drug addicts, and that some were physically or sexually abusive.

From that start, S was jettisoned into eleven years of residential school. During her involuntary confinement in residential school, she suffered physical, sexual, and psychological abuse, as well as cultural and linguistic deprivation, all of which primed her for the abusive relationship that followed.

As the Truth and Reconciliation Commission (TRC) has documented in significant detail, the kinds of abuse that S suffered in residential school are major factors that contributed to her lack of knowledge and awareness of her language and culture. They also contributed to her mistrust of authority, physical and mental health issues, criminal justice involvement, and the virtual absence of what the Correctional Service of Canada (CSC) refers to as positive 'pro-social' role models or supports.

Most of S's early charges were drug related, and like many others who experience victimization from childhood on, there were no supports provided to S to address the trauma she had experienced or prevent abuse from continuing in the future. Instead, she was introduced to substances that might temporarily anaesthetise her to her circumstances, but which ultimately heightened and exacerbated her life challenges. Her first criminal charges were intimately connected to this history and stemmed from her relationship with her abusive husband, whom she married at the age of sixteen. He introduced her to his drug-involved world.

Indigenous women now represent upward of thirty-six percent of women in Canadian federal prisons. This rate is the result of an 85.7 percent increase in the number of Indigenous women in prison over the past decade. This over representation is an ongoing legacy of Canada's racist and colonial history that traces its roots back to the breaching of Treaties, the outlawing of cultural and spiritual laws, practices and ceremonies, forced removal from lands and communities, residential schools, the so-called sixties scoop, ongoing state-sanctioned forced removal of Indigenous children from their families and communities via child-welfare interventions, inadequate living conditions and many other human rights violations, all of which have wreaked havoc in Indigenous communities and on Indigenous Peoples.

Ninety-one per cent of Indigenous women in federal prisons have experienced physical or sexual abuse, or both. Most are also poor, young, and have had access to extremely limited educational and employment opportunities.

On March 25, 2014, a psychological/psychiatric assessment summarized S's circumstances, as follows

> [S] has been continuously involved with the correctional system since age 16. She said her life "was a

> big shambles of nothing. ... I never had time to have a life," and after reviewing available information, her assessment seems accurate. While in the community, her life was dominated by alcohol and drugs, as well as petty and violent crime. While incarcerated, she was frequently involved in clashes with the system and/or clashes with other [prisoners], thus leading to volatility and deep isolation for long periods, and a resulting lack of close, stable relationships. She stated that she is "tired of being incarcerated" and wants to move forward with the rest of her life.

The story of how and why S has been criminalized and institutionalized for approximately four decades is a testament to this country's ongoing failure to ensure safety and support for Indigenous Peoples and particularly Indigenous women, as well as its failure to confront the racist and misogynist biases in Canada's justice system that still too often mean that justice is not even attempted, much less done.

S and Lorna

S currently remains imprisoned for second-degree murder resulting from the 1991 death by suicide of another prisoner, Lorna Jones, at the Prison for Women (P4W) in Kingston, Ontario. S pleaded guilty to this charge, as she did to far too many other charges while in prison. The lawyer who 'assisted' S to plead guilty to second-degree murder was subsequently disbarred because of his sexual exploitation of other women clients. S's personal feeling of guilt for what might, at most, have amounted to an assisted suicide, was far too easily accepted by all involved.

To this day, correctional staff and prisoners alike who knew Lorna and S at P4W reject that Lorna's death was anything but a suicide. By all accounts, Lorna was extremely palsied and prone to seizures, apparently as a result of a tainted dose of narcotics ingested at some point prior to her time at P4W. Yet, shockingly, Lorna was forced to rely on her fellow prisoners to help her perform the most basic functions, such as feeding, dressing, and cleaning. She and S were very close and so S was often Lorna's helper.

The staff and women at P4W, as well as the evidence considered during the inquest into her death revealed that Lorna often discussed her desire to die in the months leading up to death. In addition to her physical condition, Lorna was concerned that the increased burden of care that she required from her sister prisoners might cause resentment and result in her being alienated from them. These factors, coupled with the recent death of her brother and the suicides of a number of her friends—all but one of whom were Indigenous women in prison, more than likely contributed to what CSC labelled "her suicidal ideation."

S and Lorna were very close and considered themselves to be sisters. They both spent a lot of time in segregation and they helped each other to survive the pain and isolation of imprisonment. S helped Lorna to light cigarettes, tie her shoes, use the washroom, and although she initially refused, she says that she eventually did agree to help Lorna commit suicide.

In 1993, S reportedly admitted to a counselor that Lorna had asked her to help her commit suicide and that she had done so by helping to fashion a noose from a television cable. Sometimes, she says she helped to put the noose around Lorna's neck and tie the other end of the cable to the bars of Lorna's cell. These sorts of admissions were the primary basis for her conviction, even though police photos of the scene of Lorna's death did not match S's description. Notably, following the inquest into Lorna's death, the verdict was that the cause of death was unknown. It is nevertheless widely accepted as a suicide.

When he accepted S's plea of guilty to second-degree

murder, the judge stated that

> Lorna is dead. The authorities believed her death probably was a suicide. [S], because her conscience was bothering her, confessed to killing Lorna. If she had not done so, she would not have been charged.

Prior to her confession, S had not been charged because the evidence surrounding Lorna's death was inadequate to support her conviction. While there are inconsistencies between the accounts of the guards and S, none of the evidence points to S being responsible for Lorna's death. For instance, one guard testified that when she discovered Lorna hanging from the bars, she was unable to lift Lorna's body to relieve the pressure on her neck. S's slight frame makes it extremely unlikely that she could have hoisted Lorna's body up to hang her from the bars, particularly if Lorna was an unwilling participant being murdered.

In addition to the differences in description of the manner in which the noose was affixed to the bars, S's reproduction of the knot she claimed to have tied was inconsistent with that removed from the bars. In addition, timelines set out in CSC documents and S's own account were inconsistent. Finally, at no time since her sentencing on April 22, 1994, has the effectiveness of her legal representation been challenged. Regrettably, her lawyer has since suffered a permanently debilitating head injury.

The image that emerges is one of a criminal justice system that fails consistently to protect and treat with dignity or respect, marginalized, vulnerable and victimized Indigenous women such as Lorna and S, yet seems to spring vigorously into action to criminalize them at most opportunities. This phenomenon of under-protection and over-policing of Indigenous women, coupled with their tendency to take legal and criminal responsibility for actions that are not criminal, or which were not committed by them has been described as the hyper-responsibilization[2] of Indigenous women and is part of what also contributes to the numbers of Indigenous women who are missing and murdered in this country.

S speaks of her confession as being made while she felt intense personal guilt and responsibility to confess to a death that had been accepted as suicide. CSC's own documentation underscores the reality that its ongoing, and prolonged history of segregating S made it difficult for her to tolerate stress and stimulation. It may well have been S's conscience manifested feelings of guilt that pushed her toward a confession. While S continues to feel guilty for her actions, she no longer believes she is a murderer. Mere feelings of guilt do not and should not equate to responsibility for death, and they should not have been permitted to form the basis of her conviction for second-degree murder.

S's HISTORY REVEALS a perilous propensity for hyper-responsibilization through resignation to the unfairness of State responses to her. She has consistently conceded and accepted the consequences of charges, convictions, and sentences, without resistance. For instance, at the August 3, 1988, sentencing proceeding that commenced her current and continuing period of imprisonment, S did not heed the Saskatchewan Provincial Court judge's advice that she proceed with assistance from counsel. The judge undoubtedly recognized the minor part, if any, that S played in her husband's drug dealing, but was likely ignorant of the realistic lack of faith S and too many other Indigenous women have in a legal system that

2 "Women and the Canadian Legal System Examining Situations of Hyper-Responsibility" 26 *Canadian Woman Studies* 94. The line between moral and legal responsibility too often becomes blurred in cases involving Indigenous and other racialized women: "Canadian law is often built around expectations that individuals take responsibility for their actions and nowhere is this truer than in matters of criminal law. What we have noticed over the years is a number of situations where women (particularly when they are racialized, have a disability or a mental illness, are poor or a sexual minority) are expected by the legal system to take more responsibility than others. This is the situation we are referring to as hyper-responsibility."

delivers racism, but rarely justice. Like so many other women I know, S's response to that judge was

> I just want to get it over with, that's all. I am going to plead guilty to the charges. I know it's very serious. I've been through the system. ... I just want to get it over with you know, and cleared up, because last time I sat on remand for about eight months until I got sentenced.

She handled most other charges accumulated in prison in the same manner. Worse still, she initiated the process that resulted in the second-degree murder conviction.

S adamantly believed that she was responsible for Lorna's death. However, her personal feelings of culpability should not have resulted in a murder conviction. For S, her confession clearly alleviated her feelings of personal guilt. CSC staff recorded S's conversation with *Kingston Whig Standard* journalist Paulette Peirol, as follows

> This is very hard on me ... you know, saying I did it. But I have to get it out of my system, because if I don't, I'm a person that can't live with this for the rest of my life.

S also indicated that she thought Lorna's family could find peace if they learned that Lorna did not take her own life.

When S was informed that she may be given a life sentence for second-degree murder, she said

> I'm not even worried at this point in time, what I get, as long as I have a clear conscience and I could sleep good at night, and live with myself and love myself and like myself.

Many people, including her lawyer, agreed that she would not have been charged had she not confessed. Although, throughout its correctional files, CSC alleges that S does not take responsibility for her actions or emotions, her numerous guilty pleas to all manner of institutional and criminal charges emanating from within the multiple prison environments to which she has been subjected, including the most significant and devastating of these, her confession in relation to the death of Lorna, contradicts this assumption.

The travesty for S is not only that, without evidence from her confession, she would likely not be serving a life sentence; it is also that she is serving a life sentence with a record that, without proper context, portrays S as violent. This record resulted in S being classified as a maximum-security prisoner for most of her multiple decades in prison. For federally sentenced women, a maximum-security classification results in confinement in segregated maximum-security units within a multi-security unit within each federal prison for women. As a result of her near-constant state of segregation, S and other women classified as maximum-security prisoners end up with limited to no access to programming, educational opportunities or Indigenous ceremonies — all of which also render conditional release remote, as the lack of available opportunities to complete programs prejudices prisoners' abilities to reenter the community.[3]

Barriers to Reintegration

S's record was used again and again to maintain her security level as maximum and to segregate her, and thereby deny her access to therapeutic and rehabilitative programs and services aimed at facilitating her eventual release from prison and integration into the community. Segregation created and then exacerbated S's mental health issues and impeded her ability to recover from the many traumas of her past.

3 Office of the Correctional Investigator, *Spirit Matters: Aboriginal People and the Corrections and Conditional Release Act* (22 October 2012).

For instance, during an October 1992 Case Conference the Psychology and Psychiatry, team members working with S expressed concern regarding the "effects of extended segregation on [S's] mental health." It was recommended that she be released from prison then or at the very least, that a gradual release process be commenced post haste. I can only imagine that her life might have unfolded very differently had that recommendation been followed. Instead, S continued to serve most of her time in maximum security and to be segregated from the general prison population.

On April 22, 1994, the day that S pleaded guilty to second-degree murder, inexperienced staff at P4W intervened in a minor dispute between women in a manner that escalated the events to those which became the focus of the *Commission of Inquiry into Certain Events at the Prison for Women in Kingston* (Arbour Inquiry). S and another Indigenous woman were already in the segregation unit at P4W when six other women were dragged in, following a fracas on the range. All eight women, five of whom were Indigenous, were then subjected to what the Honourable Louise Arbour chronicled as evidence of the absence of the rule of law with respect to the treatment of federally sentenced women. The facts she documented included such unlawful actions as:

- Assaults by staff on women,
- Stripping by male staff, shackling and leaving women naked in stripped cells for days,
- Coercion to 'agree' to body cavity searches while shackled, in exchange for showers and cigarettes,
- Involuntary and unlawful transfers of women to the sex offender unit in Kingston Penitentiary for men,
- Denial of the right to counsel for more than a week,
- Unlawful segregation for ten to twelve months, and
- Coercion to enter guilty pleas to charges of attempted escape, assault and uttering threats, in order to be released from segregation.

When S eventually had access to a new, Indigenous lawyer, Don Worme, he requested that she be moved out of segregation and that her security level be reduced so that she might be held in a less restrictive environment. However, the spurious legal basis underpinning S's murder charge unduly influenced CSC staff decisions regarding rehabilitative options for S. Worse still, the correctional officer who authored S's progress report at the time noted that her transfer would assist S in avoiding responsibility for the murder of Lorna. Until she was eventually transferred to Saskatchewan, in addition to the general experiences of all of the women outlined above, generic statements of claim filed against CSC on March 5, 1998, regarding the actions of the men in the Kingston Penitentiary Institutional Emergency Response Team (IERT) at P4W on April 26, 1994, asserted that each of the women was:

- Attacked without warning by eight masked, armed men,
- Stripped naked or required to disrobe completely by the team of men,
- Placed in chains,
- Forced, naked, into the common area of the segregation unit,
- Forced to kneel, naked, for long periods of time, and
- Left chained and naked in an empty and dirty cell, the effects of which remain with her.

What is not chronicled in the legal documents, but what S told me when I saw her in the segregation cell at P4W a few days later, was that she was forced to stand in the shower area naked while restraints and shackles were fastened to her. She indicated that a male member of the team pulled back her gown and laughed at her. She also indicated that while she was held with her face against the bathroom tiles, a baton was brought up between her legs. Other women described being assaulted, having their clothes cut and ripped off of them by male staff, having requests for heart medication and sanitary products ignored, having eyeglasses smashed, and having windows being opened while the women were left shackled and naked in their cells.

When S and the other women provided the detailed accounts of what had happened to them, they also advised me that officers had video cameras and that they appeared to be filming everything that they did to the women. Neither they, nor I, knew whether the staff had actually videotaped everything they did, nor, if so, whether the videotapes still existed. When I eventually viewed the video recordings of the April 26 cell extractions, everything the women said had occurred was indeed captured on videotape, except for one important detail.

Although the video shows S being held by at least two fully armed and masked men, face to the bathroom tiles, who make odd hand motions to each other just before the tape skips ahead four minutes, neither CSC nor the video ever revealed what happened in those missing minutes. I will go to my grave believing that it was during those minutes that the baton was brought up between S's legs in the manner she described. There is no other similar skip in the tape and everything else the women reported to me is recorded. There is no other logical explanation for the skip in the videotape timer.

In order to have the shackles removed, S and the other women were required to agree to a body cavity search. Worse still, as the evidence at the Arbour Inquiry revealed, a doctor colluded with CSC by bribing women to comply with body cavity searches in exchange for a shower and a security gown. The cavity searches were completed on a dirty blanket, in a dirty cell. Although women were then placed in the shower area, they were not given enough time in the shower to wash themselves fully and then had to walk naked back to their cells before they were given clean gowns. S remembered feeling dirty, disgusted, scared, and ashamed.

Despite the numerous breaches of the law and CSC policies documented in the video, S did not lodge any complaints, nor was any disciplinary action taken against the staff in relation to the 1993 or prior incidents. She was described as having chosen not to return to Kingston to participate in the inquiry in person, although, she was so heavily medicated and isolated at Regional Psychiatric Centre (RPC) in Saskatoon, it is difficult to consider her actions as voluntary and most certainly they were not based on full information and informed consent.

In January of 1996, even though construction of the regional prison was incomplete, in an effort to draw attention away from the Arbour Inquiry's documenting of the litany of horrors of the treatment of the women at P4W, CSC decided to transfer women to the Edmonton Institution for Women (EIFW). All but one (a seventeen-year-old) of the Indigenous women transferred to Edmonton from the RPC unit were immediately segregated in the maximum-security unit, which was then euphemistically referred to as an "enhanced unit."

Parenthetically, during one of my visits to EIFW during that time, I happened to arrive at the prison at the same time as a new CSC employee. She was a social worker who I knew from the community. She was extremely excited that she was going to be working with women in the enhanced unit. She thought it was so named because the women there had access to enhanced services and supports. She had no idea that the primary enhancements in the unit were static security in nature. In fact, that first enhanced and maximum-security unit set the stage for what continues to be an ongoing status of segregation experienced by women classified as maximum-security prisoners, the majority of whom are Indigenous.

The conditions of confinement were particularly egregious for the women in the enhanced unit, but the lack of visits and programming, near constant state of lockdown, excessive and unlawful strip searches, inexperienced staff and construction-zone nature of the environment took its toll on all. Within a few months, women were fleeing the prison. Although all were easily located, usually at their homes, and one returned herself to EIFW, after three of the maximum-security women fled ten blocks before they were intercepted by police, CSC transferred all of the women to the Edmonton Remand Centre in August 1996.

A handful of women classified as minimum-security prisoners were eventually transferred back to EIFW, but all the women classified as medium and maximum security were transferred to the Saskatchewan Penitentiary (Sask Pen) — a prison for men. S and the other women would be temporarily placed at the men's penitentiary for much of the next decade, from December 1996 to February 2003.

Ineffective Grievances and Correctional Intransigence

While they were housed separately, the women's yard was visible from the men's living units and when men were moving throughout the prison yard. The men would yell obscenities at the women and unzip their pants and masturbate. When the women informed the guards, they were questioned about their behaviour and accused of enticing or otherwise provoking the men. In addition to being held responsible[4] for the men's behaviour, the women were frequently also punished by both the insinuations and by not being permitted to leave the yard until they had completed their full hour of recreation.

For most of the time the segregated maximum-security unit at Sask Pen was open, the fifteen to twenty-four women

4 The Canadian Association of Elizabeth Fry Societies (CAEFS) and the Native Women's Association of Canada (NWAC) have described this as the hyper-responsibilization of women, particularly Indigenous women. This is more fully discussed in the article, "Women and the Canadian Legal System: Examining Situations of Hyper-Responsibility" by CAEFS/NWAC, *Indigenous Women in Canada: The Voices of First Nations, Inuit and Metis Women*, Winter/Spring 2008, v. 26, n. 3,4, p. 94.

imprisoned there were almost exclusively Indigenous. Although they were told they would only be held in the men's prison for a short time and that they would have full access to programs and services, as well as Elders and spiritual and culturally specific initiatives, they actually had little access to anything but self-study with the support of a part-time educational support staff for most of their time in the segregated maximum security units.

During the eight years they were held there, the women lived two, four, or five to a range in up to seven different cell areas, with limited access to mix as a larger group. As they began to despair at never being moved out of Sask Pen, women began to self-harm at alarming rates and one woman was found hanging in her cell. As the levels of hopelessness and desperation grew, the women were encouraged by some of the men at the prison to take hostages and make demands for the programs they sought. At first, they staged hostage takings amongst themselves. When that didn't work, they started escalating their self-harming and hostage-taking.

On one visit to Sask Pen in 1999, I was called back in to the prison by the acting warden, as S had barricaded herself on the unit and because there was another woman on the range with her, she was also accused of hostage taking. The staff knew that S did not trust them and asked if I would intervene. With my then-infant daughter in a carrier, I went back in to speak with S. She was upset because staff had not followed through on their commitment to allow her to call her sister to check on the health of her father, so she refused to lock up until she could make the call. The warden allowed the call and she locked up. Despite my pleas that she go to trial and my offers to testify on her behalf, she subsequently pleaded guilty to forcible confinement and threatening assault because of her actions that evening.

During another visit a few months later, women were increasingly anxious about the ongoing paucity of programs.

After convincing four women who were segregated to file a group grievance, I proceeded to the rest of the five ranges and the hospital location to meet with twenty other women in the prison. When I was in the unit manager's office at the end of the visit, the head of security interrupted our meeting to advise that he was planning to bring in the emergency response team. I asked why. He advised that the women on the segregation tier, the first range I visited that day, were rioting — screaming, yelling threats and banging the bars of their cells. I advised that I had been down there speaking with those women a few hours before and they were upset about the lack of programming and spiritual support — they were all Indigenous — but that they were working on a group grievance to address their issues. What was striking to me was what the head of security said: "Why don't you take the baby down? I hear they like your baby." I wondered, *How serious could the risk be that the women posed if the head of security believed a baby could calm the situation? Why would they risk the potential escalation and risk of harm that accompanies engaging the riot squad?*

Massive Deterioration in Health and Mental Health

In 2005, following transfers back to EIFW from Sask Pen and then between EIFW and Philippe-Pinel Institute in Quebec, S was transferred back to RPC, which is dually designated a psychiatric hospital (pursuant to provincial health legislation) and a federal penitentiary for men. Most of her next decade would be spent there, punctuated by transfers to other prisons. In an incident on October 6, 2005, S was admitted to a hospital after being found unconscious in her RPC cell. Oversedation was deemed to be the cause of her decreased level of consciousness. She was subsequently held in ICU for eighty-four consecutive days on mechanical ventilation for adult respiratory distress syndrome and aspiration pneumonia.

Despite being in a coma and initially assessed as unlikely

to survive, S was initially placed in restraint chains and cuffed to her hospital bed. Against all odds, S survived and emerged from the coma with no memory of what had happened but overjoyed to see her sisters and nieces and nephews. I had never seen S as happy as when I entered her hospital room to see her propped up on the bed with four children cuddling, hugging, singing, and reading to her. Despite concerted efforts to argue for parole by exception for S, CSC refused to support the initiative. Instead, she was returned to RPC, re-designated as high-risk and subjected to the 'Management Protocol' a super-maximum security designation more restrictive than that in the special handling units for men considered the most violent and dangerous in Canada.

When she was finally able to exit her RPC segregation cell, predictably, the devastating impact of chronic segregation became manifest again. S exhibited extreme anxiety and sensory overload, to the point that the laughter and mouth movements of other women were intolerably stimulating and inspired crippling anxiety and paranoia.

Following the inquest into the death of Ashley Smith, with whom S was segregated in 2007, and S's residential school claim, in addition to our attempts to secure a judicial review of S's sentence and conditions of confinement, CSC began to acknowledge that since much of S's behaviour was common for people placed in segregation for inordinate amounts of time, they would be best advised to start working to assist her to get out of prison.

In March of 2015, S was transferred to the Okimaw Ohci Healing Lodge, a minimum/medium-security prison for women. A 2014 Psychological/Psychiatric Assessment Report noted that because of her history of charges in prison, S's "static risk for future violence will always be rated high" and yet stated in its conclusions that, in practice, "currently [S] presents as a low risk to reoffend violently." This contradiction highlights both how S's conditions of confinement have largely been ignored and her criminal record has been used to portray her as a risk in ways at odds with her actual behavior and interactions. The classification system has consistently discriminated against Indigenous women by over-classifying them in ways unrelated to the risk that they pose to public safety.[5]

The ongoing legacy of S's experiences at P4W are reflected today in the difficulties she faces in obtaining conditional release. Public safety is best served by supportive gradual releases, yet, as I write this, the struggle to get S out continues. She is now seventeen years past her earliest parole eligibility date. In October 2015, the Parole Board of Canada refused S's request to participate in a package of fifteen cultural and personal development ETAs (Escorted Temporary Absences) that would allow her supported, structured and supervised access to ceremonies on the Nekaneet Reserve. They did so despite acknowledging assessments that S poses a "a low risk to reoffend violently," that "global factors are assessed as low institutional adjustment, low escape risk, and low risk to the public," and importantly that her management team assessed her risk as manageable and recommended that the ETAs be authorized.

The Parole Board decision was overturned on appeal, but when they were consequently required to reassess their decision, they found as a fact that S is a violent individual and negated our attempts to obtain a royal prerogative of mercy to release her from her sentence. Rather, they labeled her a "repeat violent offender" and directed that she demonstrate a "further period of demonstrated change and compliance" just to secure an escorted pass in to the community. S's 1994 guilty plea and consequent second-degree murder conviction with respect to Lorna's death continue to be relied on to support a view of S as violent despite the reality that all who know the

5 Canadian Human Rights Commission (2003), *Protecting Their Rights*; see also, *Ewert v. R* (2015 FC 1093), now at SCC, decision pending.

circumstances view the conviction as wrongful and Lorna's death as, at most, an assisted suicide. And, virtually all of the offences committed while in prison were directly connected to periods of mental health crises.

The story that S's criminal record and files tell about her, devoid of context and assessed with tools that systematically disadvantage women and Indigenous Peoples could not be more different than how S is viewed by those who know her well. For example, a February 9, 2015 correctional assessment carried out at RPC notes that staff who have known S many years note that

> [s]he is polite and respectful toward staff and the other women. She will always step up to complete any task that is needed … is successfully able to stay out of the drama that is a daily occurrence on the women's unit. The other women look up to [her] as a model of what an individual can do when they are determined to change their lives.

Outrageously, S's ETA was also denied on the basis that she was not initially aware of the purpose of the ceremony, a give-away dance, that she had been invited to attend. Her inability to articulate the purpose of the event could be accounted for by a multitude of factors: from her dislocation from her family, community and culture, as a result of residential school and more than three decades of imprisonment; as well as her cognitive impairment and low verbal comprehension processing speed, as a result of the 2005 over-sedation while at RPC; to her discomfort, humility and nervousness during the hearing, given her lack of prior release history and extensive history of incarceration and residential school confinement.

Aside from indicating that S, "identify[ies] as an Aboriginal" and that, "[a]s a child [she] attended a residential school where [she] reportedly experienced sexual, mental physical and spiritual abuse, as well as starvation and neglect," the Parole Board failed to consider the implications of those circumstances for S as is required by section 718(2)(e) of the *Criminal Code.*

Instead, Parole Board members disrespectfully derided S's ignorance and confusion. The Truth and Reconciliation Commission recognized cultural disconnection as contributing significantly to victimization and criminalization of individuals like S. S's experiences, ones shared by too many Indigenous women, were approached not as needs that the criminal justice system must respond to, but as risks requiring caution, concern for safety, and punishment.

THE HONOURABLE LOUISE ARBOUR has called for the elimination of segregation for women, a call that has been echoed by the Canadian Association of Elizabeth Fry Societies, the Native Women's Association of Canada, the Canadian and Ontario Human Rights Commissions and the DisAbled Women's Network of Canada. This call reflects both the inherent harm of segregation, which the UN Special Rapporteur on Torture has declared can constitute torture, and the added, discriminatory impact of segregation on women, particularly Indigenous women and those with mental health issues, both of whom are disproportionately and unjustly labelled as security risks, with no apparent regard for the impact of disabling mental health issues and past trauma resulting from abuse.

S has experienced the worst of our education, mental health and prison systems. Her life has been a litany of the failures of Canada when it comes to Indigenous women. The abuse that she suffered at the hands of virtually every man, and later every state actor in her life, have resulted in her continued marginalization, repeated victimization, and incessant criminalization and imprisonment.

I will not rest until S is both freed from her incarceration and exonerated for the death of Lorna Jones. She has survived most of her family. The least we can do is to make room for her to experience the dignity of her last few years with those who love and care for her.

Jennifer Briscoe was called to the Ontario Bar in 1985 and the Quebec Civil Bar in 1988. She served as a Prosecutor for the Dept. of Justice in Ottawa then Montreal as well as a member of the Flying Team in Canada's North. She was onsite legal advisor for the Toronto Police Service and Counsel in complex mega prosecutions. She currently serves as an agent for the Public Prosecution Service of Canada.

Jennifer Briscoe

Fly-In Justice in the North

I STOOD THERE. The darkness was overwhelming, no cars, no lights, no sound. It was hard to believe we had flown several hours north from what seemed a very northerly point of our country. It was still dark at 8:30 a.m.

The silence was absolute, broken only by the crisp sounds of our footsteps on the snow as we slowly moved from the plane across the landing strip.

I will never forget the feeling that I had been transported to another world. I soon realized that in many ways I had. The Department of Justice Fly-In Squad had arrived at Old Crow in the Yukon Territory, north of the Arctic Circle. It was mid-October, yet winter had arrived. The silhouette of innumerable crows could be made out, perched atop the snow-covered roofs of the houses. As we approached, large flocks of them lifted off and scattered — the only other sound in what was a deafening silence. The town was still asleep.

As daylight began to emerge, I was struck with the beauty of Old Crow's log cabins, some of them with drying furs and caribou carcasses neatly hanging outside. The cabins and town were surrounded by trees and bush, a surprising and unexpected sight for me this far north.

"Go North!"

Back when I started at the Department of Justice, several senior counsel gave me the same advice about practicing criminal law. "Go North," they'd say, meaning that if I experienced criminal law in small remote communities, I would get a practical understanding of criminal justice and its impact from an up-close and personal perspective. It would also test my creativity in applying the law, they suggested.

The Fly-In team, as it was called, was comprised of a judge, defence counsel, Crown counsel, court reporter, clerk and translator. It was, in essence, a travelling Criminal Justice Court serving Canada's remote Northern communities. As soon as I was offered the opportunity to assist in the North, I jumped at the chance.

My first trip was to Whitehorse in the Yukon. The city of Whitehorse is a spectacularly beautiful corner of this exceptional country I call home. The courthouse was relatively new and the lawyers' lounge looked out over a snow-peaked mountain range. It felt surreal that I could retreat to this place between court breaks. It was glorious and meditative. Up until that time, my practice had been confined to big city courthouses in Ottawa, Montreal, and Toronto. I was unfamiliar with either living in or practicing law in a small community. Moreover, the presence and influence, the art and lifestyle of our First Nations people was far more evident.

I made several trips to Whitehorse before I was asked to handle the circuit court in Old Crow, a community that could only be reached by plane, some eight-hundred kilometers north of there. The pilot re-arranged our seating and court bags to even out the weight in the plane. It occurred to me there was some danger in what I had undertaken. Having just returned safely from a weekend hiking trip though Kluane National Park, with bear sightings but no incidents, I wondered if I was pushing my luck. As it turns out, this experience had an indelible impact on my life and career and changed the way I practiced law.

Being part of the Fly-In team, as I was on many occasions over the next thirty years, is a life-changing experience for every participant, most certainly for me as Crown counsel. I soon learned that preconceptions and big city procedures are best left on the airplane. So here I was in Old Crow.

Our first stop was the RCMP station, a small outpost nothing like the big city counterparts. As we entered the building, I observed a large plastic bin filled with empty alcohol bottles. I learned the town was a dry community and these bottles represented the recent seizures from unregulated bootleggers. This prohibition was not uncommon in some communities in the North, often welcomed by them.

On the morning of trial, the RCMP travelled around the village rousing and ensuring attendance of participants in the criminal process. Court started when the police signalled that the majority had gathered. The octagonal-shaped community centre at the heart of the town was transformed into a courtroom with photos of the Elders lining the walls and gazing down upon us. The makeshift courtroom became a community theatre.

As court unfolded, many in the community were there to watch. One learns quickly to discard the city scripts. Measurement of time and distance are irrelevant in communities with no street signs, few points of reference, and a vast emptiness, often with little daylight as we know it.

One also learns to embrace common sense. In the first

case I prosecuted in Old Crow, an accused had discharged a firearm at another. Identification of the perpetrator was in issue and I asked the victim witness, "Can you please indicate if you see the person you described present before the Court?" Once translated, the witness looked quizzically at me and responded, "Don't you?" The laughter was far from muted and I cringed at how silly my question must have sounded.

The Court is important whether makeshift or not. Few are not affected by its presence in their town. Many in the community attend and put their everyday tasks on hold, but only to a degree.

A woman's husband had been charged with assault causing bodily harm. He had chopped her thumb off in a fit of rage during an argument. Despite the fact that she did not wish to testify against him, the charge was serious and her injuries severe enough that she had to be flown to Whitehorse for surgery and treatment.

We began the case. It was very difficult with a reluctant witness who was torn between her wish to protect her husband and the fact that she was testifying before many in the community who knew the truth about their relationship. Suddenly, in the middle of the trial, someone burst into the makeshift courtroom. In the chaos, the Court learned that a canoe had tipped while crossing the Porcupine River and that a child had fallen into the water along with his grandfather. The trial was no longer relevant as the courtroom emptied. By chance, our Fly-In team's presence offered an opportunity for rescue. The pilot, standing by until court ended, was seconded to encircle the area to search for the lost child. Sadly the search was in vain, night fell early in this area of the world. The Court did not resume, the pilot returned, and we all took some time to recompose. We left at day's end, a docket unfinished, a community in shock and in mourning.

My next series of circuits to the Arctic Circle took me to various communities in Nunavut — all unique and different, yet somehow linked by a strong connection to the land. Igloolik is located on a small island in Foxe Basin off the northern tip of Melville Peninsula in Nunavut, another community served only by air. At the time, the population hovered at about 1,200 persons.

As the Fly-In team 'visited', life unfolded in another makeshift courtroom. Not unlike communities everywhere, one finds that mental illness, strained interpersonal relations, and occasional tragedy are not strangers to the experiences of circuit court members.

I was prosecuting a woman I will call Susie who was charged with several serious firearms offences. Her brother, concerned that she was armed and was going to hurt herself — as she had threatened to do and, in fact, had done in the past — called the RCMP detachment there to assist.

As they arrived, they were careful in their approach to the house. They were familiar with Susie's erratic and unstable predicament and they also knew that a hunting rifle would be on the premises. She began threatening and firing at them. They backed away, hiding behind their vehicles until eventually she was subdued and controlled. No one was hurt. After her arrest, she was denied bail as no one came forward or was able to offer assistance. She seemed rootless, a stranger among her own. In this and other communities, Susie had a history of erratic behavior and criminal misconduct. She was deemed a risk to herself and others. Many had tried to help but she was on a road to self-destruction. The community could not absorb the threat she presented and she was seen as an outsider. A conviction would mean she would be sent to a major city in the south to serve a jail sentence. This, I was told, distressed her even more than any conviction.

There was a concern, of course, of mental illness and instability that soon played out. Facing several charges and unable to assist legal counsel in establishing a defence, the judge bifurcated his decision, finding her not guilty on one charge but guilty on the others. As judgment was being passed, she suddenly wailed and grabbed a pen from her counsel's hand and began stabbing herself in the neck. It was horrible for all of us assembled there. It was clear that her mental illness had never been adequately addressed. I suspected the reasons for that were the lack of infrastructure and services in the remote communities, coupled with her inability to stay in any one place long enough to get proper help.

One can only imagine the impact her violent actions had on those gathered in the makeshift courthouse that day. That impact became demonstratively real for one young six-year-old girl who'd learned of it, while sitting patiently in a waiting area just outside the courtroom.

This young girl was the victim of sexual abuse and the main witness to testify in the next case on the docket. While the neck-stabbing drama unfolded, she waited for her case to be heard. Traumatized by the screaming and shouting that she could hear from the courtroom, she was speechless and unable to participate. That case was no more. Regrettably, it would have to wait until the next circuit. I hoped that the time and distance from these events would give this young girl a chance to recuperate her faith and trust.

I INITIALLY PONDERED, as we 'visited' remote villages, whether it was appropriate to impose 'a white man's justice' on a community that might just not need us. It often crossed my mind that we may seem a little like aliens landing, striking fear and at times incomprehension as we went about our business, sometimes even carrying people off with us to far places. As it turns out, the fact that convicted persons would face a jail sentence 'south' was often determinative of a witness's cooperation. I sensed that these witnesses were credible and were telling the truth, but that they could not live with the outcome of contributing to a conviction. It was not uncommon to have a woman refuse to testify against a partner based on the fact he was the hunter and the family depended on him for their food.

As I became more experienced, my opinion gradually shifted, especially in relation to women who were victims of repetitive violence — unprotected without outside intervention of the rule of law. It became obvious that for many women, we provided a safety net where one did not exist.

To bring a sense of accountability and protection to an otherwise helpless victim became a major *raison d'etre*. This was brought home to me on a particularly significant day in the Igloolik courtroom. A grandmother who was raising her six-year-old grandaughter appeared before us. Grandparents raising children was not unusual in many communities where shared-raising of an oldest child is quite common. However, this particular child was the subject of abuse by her grandfather. The grandmother had been incredibly supportive in encouraging, yet protecting the child as a witness.

The grandmother worked with the RCMP with dignity and resolve knowing that our system would try to intervene to stop the abuse. Notwithstanding her efforts to protect the child against her husband, she understood she could not do this on her own. Working through a translator, she explained she had watched her otherwise-cheerful grandaughter suddenly change into a sad and anxious girl. Eventually, her granddaughter had confided the details of her grandfather's transgressions. She was angry, outraged and helpless to do anything without the intervention of the RCMP.

Susie's courtroom drama tragically prevented the resolution on that day for the family, but their willingness to access the justice system was demonstrative and reassuring. There was, it seemed, a breaking point when the criminal justice system could help.

Iqaluit was the most southerly city of Baffin Island that I visited. On my first winter visit, I was outfitted with a government issue Canada Goose jacket, an excursion coat available for staff to wear years before they became a status symbol. I would need it to brave the winter weather and winds. Juxtaposed against the small communities scattered around Nunavut, I came to think of Iqaluit as 'the big smoke'. Equipped with grocery stores, art gallery, hotels, movie theatre, coffee shops and restaurants and eventually even traffic lights, it was a bustling busy place. At times we returned from circuits at night, the city was ablaze with lights after hours of flying in darkness. It was here that I saw my first display of northern lights.

I did many cases over the years in Iqaluit. The assortment of witnesses and attitudes was diverse. Often times, I experienced an inexplicable and strange energy. For instance, I had a case involving a serious assault. While I was interviewing the victim, in passing he removed his hat and displayed horrible zigzag scars across his scalp. He had previously been attacked by a polar bear while out on the land. This assault by another male person became, in context, child's play. It really was insignificant to him, yet he showed up to testify. Interestingly, I learned later that Inuit who have survived bear attacks take on an aura and indeed special status in the folklore of their culture.

Taloyoak is the northernmost community of Canada's mainland, located on the south-western coast of Boothia Peninsula at the Northwest Passage in Nunavut. Like Iqaluit, Taloyoak is another community served only by air. At the time, its population hovered at about one thousand persons.

Remarkably, Taloyoak features 24-hour sunlight each day from May until the end of July. I visited during that time and experienced the phenomena of working until two a.m. and walking back to my room in daylight. I even saw children outside playing at that strange hour. It was actually energizing to have 24 hours of sunlight.

I remember going for a long walk with one of the women in the community who assisted with witnesses and victims. She walked me along the rolling dark tundra and rocky terrain to a gallery where the women made and sold their colorful traditional parkas or *amautiit* as well as their packing dolls made from boiled wool. She talked of the isolation, which she both loved but was, at times, frustrated by. The fragility of life in Taloyoak was striking, but these women were survivors and gathered often to support each other. I was left with an amazing feeling of the power of these women in their community.

Pond Inlet is situated on the northern tip of Baffin Island near the Eastern entrance to the Northwest Passage. It overlooks Eclipse Sound and the mountains of Bylot Island, which features a bird sanctuary.

My circuit to Pond Inlet was the most northernly and by far the coldest location I experienced — February being brutally cold that far above the Arctic Circle. We travelled commercial airline there, carrying with us a hockey-bag full of the week's docket and trials. The docket was voluminous owing to the previous circuit having been cancelled as a result of inclement weather. Plumbing problems at the Tununiq Sauniq Co-Op bumped my co-counsel out of her room and into the RCMP no-frills visiting quarters for a few days. In the ten-minute walk from the Co-Op to the RCMP station, we saw kids happy and playing in the snow oblivious to what was most certainly life-threatening cold. With the wind chill factor, the temperature dropped at night to -50 degrees C. We made that trip as few times as possible.

The first day of court, I mentioned to the witness/victim support worker that my fingers had frozen in the brief trek from the Co-op to the recreational hall where court was convening. She promptly introduced me to a spectator in the court who measured my hands and returned to court the next day with fox-trimmed sealskin mittens, made to measure.

Amongst the many trials, I handled an impaired driving case I will never forget. There was no Breathalyzer or blood test in the case but the facts involved the accused who had been reported by a witness to be driving his vehicle erratically and had almost crashed. The witness knew the accused, so the RCMP attended immediately at the accused's house. They pulled up behind him just as he stopped his vehicle. In his haste to disassociate himself from his vehicle, he had jumped from it without properly putting it in park. The truck continued on its route until one of the officers was able to stop it before it made its course down the fairly steep escarpment that abuts and forms part of the hamlet. The accused testified and admitted he had been drinking but insisted he had only had a few drinks and was not impaired.

He maintained he and his drinking buddy had even left a few ounces in the bottle they had opened that day. He said he was sober enough to drive, proof being he had not passed out. He wasn't really able to explain why he jumped from and left his truck running without placing it in park. The only cross-examination I had for him was to clarify the amount of alcohol consumed; three to four highball glasses without mix within a short time frame. Ironically for me, it was almost disheartening to have an accused render what appeared to be a truthful account yet not be able to raise a reasonable doubt. I think I actually regretted prosecuting him. However, earlier that week the RCMP had driven me up to the top of this escarpment so I could take pictures of the stunning view of Eclipse Sound and the mountains on Bylot Island. It was alarming to think what might have happened had that truck continued on its driverless course.

I HAVE MANY MEMORIES of places like Rankin Inlet, Cambridge Bay and Hall Beach, which were among the towns, or hamlets I visited as part of the Fly-In team. On many occasions, I also had the opportunity to prosecute cases in Yellowknife, a fascinating and diverse city, and a microcosm of our country. A growing city with a French community and impressive amenities, yet on the doorstep to remote Indigenous communities served by the circuit court.

The trips to the North were both exhilarating and terrifying. The need to get it right, to find the balance in the so-called search for the truth while respecting the dignity of those in the process and community was all encompassing. I could prepare for my trials, know the evidence and applicable law but this forum in the North had many intangibles. It was so important to make and leave the right impression. I was part of the criminal justice system that flew in and flew out, leaving behind much to be talked about. We hit the ground running and as I came to describe my criminal work experience, the North was also where the rubber hit the road.

Many of the people up there know one another. The complexity of prosecuting cases in the North is connected to the concern that what is said in a courtroom would affect the community. While as lawyers we are used to being recorded with our words serving to create a record, all this pales with the thoughts being recorded in the minds of community members who are present in the courtroom. Unlike in the big city where high school classes or the odd curious observer come to witness high profile cases unless they are the parties or supportive family members, in the North, court proceedings are attended by many who feel they and their community have a stake in what is to happen.

My experiences serving as Crown prosecutor in the North have changed my life, my relationships and my view of criminal justice. Elders are the core of each community there. They embody, preserve, and enhance the culture and important traditions. They are the key to any acceptance of a circuit court. Learning to respect them enhances respect for the rule of law being viable in their communities. I can't help but think of how often in criminal justice 'in the south' — in the big cities — the demonstrative absence of an 'Elder' results in the missing compass in many lives.

Moreover, prosecuting in the North brings into focus the importance and success of sentencing circles in an age of the increasing need for restorative justice everywhere in Canada.

The RCMP are often included in the criticism of police forces in general, but they perform a remarkable and enlightened role in the communities of the North. Where they are embedded, they are respectful and respected. Their investment in serving, as well as protecting, is enormously important and commendable. In more than one community, I experienced RCMP partners and families opening their homes to Indigenous people to assist in educating and life skills, where needed. From tutoring to cooking classes to art lessons, they blend in with the communities. It is remarkable to see this accommodation of different cultures.

THE LANDSCAPES OF THE NATION find their art galleries in the North. The beauty of its changing terrain from vast and seemingly lonely prairies of snow and ice to the glacial lakes and powerful escarpments is breathtaking.

Unhindered horizons exist in these places. The sky is voluminous and the world sometimes appears flat.

The cold and the adaption to it, the silent darkness, and the heavenly galaxies are carved into and shape your spiritual connection to the earth. The people of the North, their respect for traditions, their love and respectful use of their natural resources, their ingenuity and their generosity of spirit can never be forgotten by anyone who experiences it.

As I write this chapter, I am struck by the remarkable acceptance of the Fly-In Court in the communities we visited and, I might add, of me as a woman practicing criminal law. In our big cities, if I may generalize, the criminal justice system and the Court is shunned, isolated, avoided, and misunderstood. It exists apart from everyday community life. In the North on the other hand, it reverberates and is felt by the many who gather to witness the account of the events. There are no secrets, no strangers, and no isolation. It is a part of life. Failure is accepted, in some way, as universal. Accountability, engagement, and restorative justice are essential to the community's wellbeing. It taught me so much.

On a mantle in my home is a sculpture that an Igloolik artist, Marius Kayotak, made for me; a dancing drummer — proud and fierce. I see it every day and it reminds me somehow of justice in the far North of this great land. It is not blindfolded, it does not carry a scale or a sword rather it is rooted, treading the land while singing and celebrating.

Catherine Dunn received her LL.B from the University of Manitoba and has practiced law for forty years. She is Co-Chair of the Child Protection Defence Lawyers Association and is past Chair of Ikwe-Widdjiitiwin Inc., an Indigenous women's domestic abuse shelter in Manitoba. Catherine is an originating member of 'Jumping Through Hoops', a study that examined the experiences of Indigenous mothers involved with child welfare and the legal system.

Catherine Dunn

Silent Partner

When I first meet Anna (a pseudonym), she is extremely withdrawn and reserved. I am a stranger to her as she has had no previous contact with the justice system. Anna is understandably wary of me. Initially she does not look at me, or speak to me and when asked, she provides only the briefest responses, averting her gaze and often covering her mouth with her hand as she speaks. I try to establish a rapport with her, sharing that I too am the mother of a toddler; speaking to her as gently as I can about her background. I explain the charge against her, the court process, and the consequences of a conviction. The facts are extremely serious. Anna is being prosecuted by indictable offence, which carries a maximum of five years in the penitentiary. Here are the details as I saw them.

Anna's Story

It is 1987. The last Indian residential school will not close in Canada until 1996. Battered Wife Syndrome has yet to be validated by the Supreme Court of Canada. It will be decades before domestic violence, child welfare, and criminal justice will be judicially linked to historical and cultural oppression created by the impact of settler colonialism.

Anna looks younger than she is, a prisoner's grey sweatshirt dwarfing her tiny frame. Blue nylon boots issued by the Winnipeg Remand Centre hang off her feet. Her straight black hair falls over her face, her cheek and jaw are bruised and swelling like a snake bite, squeezing her eye shut while leaking blood and water. Anna has been charged with "fail to provide the necessaries of life" pursuant to Section 215(1) of the *Criminal Code*. She has failed to seek medical treatment for her nine-month-old daughter, now dead from complications as a result of a blunt trauma injury to the abdomen.

Anna has been flown to Winnipeg from Bloodvein, a Treaty 5 Reserve located on the eastern shore of Lake Winnipeg and home to Ojibwa hunters, fishers, and gatherers. The reserve is surrounded by the largest untouched boreal forest in the world. Local rock art (petroglyphs) date back over a thousand years. Despite a rich and proud history, Bloodvein, like many reserves, is challenged by third-world poverty, poor housing, lack of infrastructure, and paralyzing unemployment. In order to 'kill the Indian in the child', residents of Bloodvein, like residents of many reserves across the country, were forced to attend Indian residential schools, a policy initiated by the Canadian Government in the nineteenth century. As has been well-documented through the Truth and Reconciliation Commission, these schools had devastating social and cultural consequences which continue to have a direct impact on First Nations people today.

Anna and her domestic partner, Felix (also a pseudonym) originally meet in Winnipeg, having come from separate reserves in northern Manitoba. Anna was born in a reserve but raised in Winnipeg, in foster care. Shortly after they meet, they return to live on Felix's reserve in Bloodvein where they have three children, ages three, two, and nine months on the date of the offence. Anna lacks a strong connection with Felix's community and has few formal or informal resources on which to rely. Through Felix she is able to obtain housing and band assistance, but has limited social contact, relying primarily on the women in Felix's family. Anna does not drive, does not have easy access to transportation, is often without a phone, has no access to daycare, has no control over the family's finances, and does not have contact with her own family of origin, having been placed in foster care at an early age.

Her partner Felix has a significant alcohol problem. He has a criminal record, including assault, and has a reputation in the community for raging alcohol-fuelled encounters resulting in injuries to other people and damage to property. Anna's medical file shows a steady stream of contact with the local nursing station for injuries for which no cause is ever recorded. Her injuries include broken bones, smashed teeth, and black eyes. Nothing in the medical file suggests that her partner is responsible, and there are no complaints by Anna against him to the Band Constable or to the local RCMP. There is no therapist or mental health worker on reserve, nor is there a domestic violence shelter. Anna has no safe space in which to go, and in the time up to and including the birth of her daughter, Anna lives in a world of complete isolation, combined with a daily fear of being physically assaulted. In the dangerous world created by her partner for herself and her children, her silence is the only way in which to survive.

Anna has an exemplary parenting history. Medical reports from the nursing station confirm that she has taken her infant daughter, as well as her other children, regularly for medical check-ups. Her infant is up to date on her vaccinations and is meeting her milestones for height, weight, and development. Any small health concerns, such as colds or fevers, are attended to promptly. There is no concerning medical history with respect to her two older children. After the death of her infant daughter, an autopsy confirms that the infant presents as a healthy, nourished baby with no unusual unhealed and unreported fractures, bruising or other issues. Anna has no history of alcohol abuse, does not have a criminal record, and has no apparent mental health issues. Although rarely seen in the community, Anna is considered to be law abiding. She spends most of her time in the family home and is only seen in the community accompanied by her three children, all of whom are bonded with her. By contrast, Felix spends much of his time away from the home, is often intoxicated in public, and is either the perpetrator or recipient of many assaults. Bloodvein is a dry reserve.

After the death of their infant daughter, both Felix and Anna are charged with failing to provide the necessaries of life. Felix's charge is dropped after the preliminary hearing as he has a partial alibi. In the hours leading up to the injury to the infant daughter, Felix, who is in his early thirties, is found at a teenage drinking party taking place on the shores of Lake Winnipeg.

None of the information with respect to the hours preceding the injury and death of her infant daughter is provided directly to me by Anna, who remains mostly silent throughout my interaction with her over the next twelve months. Confirming she was with her daughter at all relevant times, she does not explain what she knows or doesn't know about the injuries received by her daughter. She does not comment on her role or understanding of those injuries and never at any time does she suggest that Felix was involved or responsible in any way for her own facial injuries noted at the time of her arrest or for the injuries which resulted in the death of her daughter. Anna does not explain why she failed to obtain medical intervention for her daughter, despite clear forensic evidence that her daughter would have been in obvious distress from blunt force injury to her abdomen, and which may have been intentional.

What Happened?

Although Anna never reveals what happened on the night in question, she slowly, and over a period of a year, provides me with a glimpse of her domestic life with Felix. She shares that on one occasion after being assaulted by Felix, who was in an alcoholic rage, she runs barefoot in her nightdress to her mother-in-law's home approximately three kilometers away. It is a cool September night in northern Manitoba. Anna arrives at the home, and despite the fact that she can both hear and see people laughing within the residence, no one answers her knock or her pleas for help. Afraid to go back home, Anna makes the decision to spend the cold night on her mother-in-law's wooden stoop. On another occasion, and prior to her baby's birth, Anna describes having been forced to flee from Felix's wrath by running into the bush and hiding there, silent and shivering, while her husband searches for her, rifle in hand. None of these incidences of domestic violence are ever reported. It is never suggested by Anna, to myself, or to police, that in the hours preceding the death of her daughter, that Felix is responsible for her facial injuries or the injuries to her daughter.

When Anna is released on bail, she is permitted to remain in Winnipeg, subject to a reporting condition and never returns to Bloodvein or to reside with her common-law partner. Her two children remain in foster care in Bloodvein, having been apprehended by Child and Family Services. On social assistance, and reporting regularly to her probation officer as a condition of her recognizance, Anna lives trouble free on bail in Winnipeg.

The preliminary hearing is held in Bloodvein at the local Band Office. All of the court staff flies in from Winnipeg for the hearing. The judge is a white male, the Crown attorney is a white male, the court clerk is a white male, the RCMP officers providing evidence are white males, the primary Crown witness, a forensic pathologist, is a white male. The court audience observing the preliminary hearing are predominantly male, and are either members or friends of Felix's family. As per court protocol, there was never any communication, conversation or direct contact between court staff and my client other than with respect to her election to seek a Queen's Bench trial. It is unnerving for Anna to participate in the judicial process. Other than this incident, she has never had contact with the police nor with the court system and its customs are alien to her.

The evidence at the preliminary hearing confirms that Anna frantically called for a medical transportation vehicle in the early morning hours regarding her daughter, who is unresponsive, cold to the touch. She does not complain about her infant being in obvious distress at any time (in contrast to the medical examiner's evidence about the consequences of the injury). Her partner is not home and the only other adult in the home is Anna. She is described as appropriately shocked and disturbed by the condition of her daughter as she attends with transportation personnel to the nursing station. Upon arrival, the infant is pronounced dead, and in the beginning stages of rigor mortis. Anna is described as inconsolable with grief. RCMP officers who return with her to her home note that the condition of the home is neat and tidy, the cupboards are well stocked with food and baby supplies, and upon arrival, medical personnel note that the two other children are asleep and otherwise unharmed.

The primary Crown evidence is provided by the medical

examiner, a forensic pathologist. His evidence confirms that the location of the infant's injuries is concerning. The medical examiner was emphatic that the injuries could not have resulted as a result of the infant being dropped or the result of an accidental fall. The force was applied directly to the abdomen. The infant would have been in considerable visible and audible distress for a number of hours preceding her death. The autopsy report prepared by the medical examiner concluded that as a result of blunt trauma to the child's abdomen, her bowel ruptured and the contents excreted into her blood system, eventually causing sepsis and death. As a mother myself, it was difficult for me to understand why any mother would not seek medical treatment for their infant daughter in the circumstances. Given Anna's excellent parenting history, it did not make sense to me that she would make a conscious, or even an unconscious decision to allow her daughter to suffer in such an agonizing way.

Coming to Anna's story from a place of privilege made it difficult for me to appreciate Anna's circumstances. Her life experiences and mine were vastly different. On an intellectual level, I could recognize Anna's circumstances as difficult and often bizarre; emotionally I had no real understanding of her day-to-day challenges. As a mother, I was deeply aware of the strong instinct to protect one's children at all costs. It did not seem possible from Anna's strong parenting record that she would deliberately choose to fatally delay medical treatment for her baby. As a lawyer, I was aware that difficult circumstances often produce difficult results. Fear, anger, even resentment can create complex psychological perceptions and conduct which subjectively seem inexplicable. As a woman living in financial, physical, and emotional security, it was impossible for me to comprehend, at a gut level, the daily challenges which Anna lived and which I never experienced.

In the months and years leading up to this tragedy, Anna lived a life of complete physical and emotional isolation. Her day-to-day survival was dependent on the behaviour of a domestic partner who was at times withdrawn and at other times unpredictable and explosive. I have, over the course of my career, seen hundreds of women living with the effects of domestic violence. They come from all walks of life, all cultural groups and all socio-economic groups. Without exception, they articulate a sense of powerlessness about their situations. They believe their partners have complete control over their lives and their bodies. Even when physically separated, they continue to be subjugated by the power they perceive their abusers have, notwithstanding that they no longer live together as a couple. They struggle to appreciate that their legal rights are to protect them and not to protect their partner. They perceive their partner's legal authority to be bigger, stronger, and more oppressive than their own. They often feel that their own conduct is directly related to the negative consequences from which they suffer. It can take months, or even years, to erase the effects of even short periods of a cohabitation that is marred by domestic violence.

The image of Anna hiding in the bush, prior to her infant's birth, as her partner hunted her methodically through the night, and the equally disturbing image of her then nine-month-old baby needlessly suffering for hours prior to her death, was distressing. Anna at no time made a connection of any kind between her own dangerous situation and what happened to her daughter. What happened that night in the early hours preceding her daughter's death, I will never know. While Anna's partner was absent for a significant portion of the preceding twenty-four hours in which her daughter was injured, Anna was in attendance and present in the home for the entire period preceding and subsequent to the injury and death of her of daughter.

Legal Issue

The *Criminal Code* provides that every parent, foster parent, and guardian, or head of the family is obligated to provide the necessaries of life for a child under the age of sixteen years, including medical treatment. The section imposes a legal duty. The personal characteristics of the defendant, falling short of mental capacity to appreciate the risk, are not relevant. The *Criminal Code* imposes liability on an objective basis and considers what the accused ought to have known. The Court must consider the conduct of a reasonable parent in relation to the facts of the case.

Anna's case was resolved approximately twelve months after the offence by way of a guilty plea before a Winnipeg Court of Queen's Bench judge. Because of the serious nature of the case, the Crown was seeking a three-year penitentiary term. It was the defence's position that Anna was not a candidate for the penitentiary, based on her lack of record and difficult history. The Court accepted a three-year period of probation on condition that she successfully complete a counselling program to be completed at an Aboriginal Healing Centre located in Selkirk, Manitoba. To my knowledge, Anna has never returned to the criminal justice system either as a victim or as a perpetrator.

Exactly how her infant daughter came to be injured and why obvious medical treatment was never sought was not resolved through the Court process. It is possible that Anna, frustrated with her life of isolation and resentful of her partner, did not pursue medical treatment out of fear for her own actions. It is possible that her partner was responsible for the injuries to her daughter and given his penchant for violence, he threatened Anna if she sought assistance. Perhaps both parents were responsible for the injuries but subjectively did not appreciate the urgency of the situation. The latter scenario is not a defence. The legal requirement to seek medical treatment is based on the objective test: what a reasonable parent would know and would do in the circumstances. Given the evidence of the forensic pathologist, Anna would have objectively known her daughter needed medical treatment.

The criminal justice system now recognizes domestic violence as a substantial and serious issue.

> The gravity, indeed, the tragedy of domestic violence can hardly be overstated. Greater media attention to this phenomenon in recent years has revealed both its prevalence and its horrific impact on women from all walks of life.[1]

In 1991, Canada ratified Article 19(1) of the *Convention on the Rights of the Child*, and imposed an obligation on participants to

> ...take all appropriate legislative, administrative, social and educational measures to protect the child from all forms of physical or mental violence, injury or abuse, neglect or negligent treatment, maltreatment or exploitation, including sexual abuse, while in the care of parent(s), legal guardian(s) or any other person who has the care of the child."

The Province of Manitoba specifically endorses this declaration.

It is an understatement to say that children and vulnerable adults such as Anna need greater support in the justice system. Anna's failure to provide medical necessities for her daughter may well have been the result of a desperate situation commencing months or even years leading up to this tragic event. Had Anna had access to justice-based, federally funded community programming, this tragedy may have been averted.

1 Wilson, J. in *R. v. Lavallee* 1990 CanLii 95 (SCC), [1990] 1 S.C.R. 852.

The failure of an otherwise competent and loving mother to protect her daughter in a culture that honours children above all else must be viewed in part through the lens of history and the ramifications of Indian residential schools. Felix, the child of a residential school survivor, was not exposed as a child to appropriate parenting in his own childhood and experienced and witnessed domestic violence in his home. Lack of education, employment and family of origin issues played a part in his addiction to alcohol and his subsequent inability to care appropriately for his partner and his children.

Systemic Change

Not much has changed since Anna was charged. First Nations communities still have little or no funding or assistance in dealing with domestic violence on reserves. There are few communities that have mental health therapists, domestic abuse counsellors, designated safe spaces, or access to those services that protect women and children from domestic violence. Few reserves have access to alcohol treatment centres on site. Many communities have only a single NDAP (Native Drug and Alcohol Program) worker in the community to assist members with alcohol and drug addictions. Privacy and anonymity is difficult on reserve, a key component of AA philosophy. Waiting lists for treatment outside the reserves are significant and often after-care programming on reserves are scarce. Overcrowding and inadequate housing create an unhealthy environment for domestic conflict which, over time, can become domestic abuse. Funding for early education and daycares which would permit parents some flexibility in child-care is inadequate. Many reserves cannot afford to provide prevention services through its child welfare agencies,thereby placing young families at risk. As a result of inequities in the federal funding model, child welfare cases attracting child protection issues are funded more robustly than prevention cases. Despite overwhelming evidence that prevention is the key to ending child welfare issues, the Federal Government has been reluctant to recognize the importance of child welfare prevention funding on First Nations. I strongly believe that the presence of some or all of these resources would have prevented the death of this innocent baby and the loss of her two siblings to child welfare.

Currently, there are more Indigenous children in foster care in Manitoba than were in residential schools in the province during any given year. On January 31, 2014, a three-volume Commission of Inquiry report entitled *The Legacy of Phoenix Sinclair: Achieving The Best For All Our Children* was released by the Honourable Commissioner Ted Hughes. At the time, I was acting as Intervener Counsel on behalf of a community-based Indigenous organization during two of the three phases of the Commission Hearing. The Inquiry resulted from the 2005 death of Phoenix Sinclair, a toddler in foster care who was systematically physically abused, starved, and eventually murdered by her mother and step-father after she was returned to them by child welfare.

The Commission of Inquiry commenced in March 2011 and was one of the longest and most expensive inquiries in Manitoba history, at a cost of $14 million. The Inquiry focused on the child welfare system in Manitoba. At its conclusion, Commissioner Hughes made sixty-two child welfare reform recommendations. Specifically, he recommended that long-term funding for community-based organizations be funded by the Federal and Provincial Government agencies to permit families to obtain support to community-based programming in their home communities that would address early child welfare prevention by including enriched early education programming for First Nations children. It is important to note that the Federal Government refused to participate in the Commission for Inquiry notwithstanding that they are the legal and exclusive funders of Indigenous children on First Nations.

The report noted that there were, at the time of the Inquiry, ten thousand children in care in Manitoba, an estimated eighty-five percent of whom were Indigenous. Four years later, the 2018 statistics confirm that there are now eleven thousand children in foster care in Manitoba, ninety percent of whom are Indigenous. That is considerably more than were in residential schools in Manitoba at their peak during the late 1950s. Unfortunately most of these children come into care as a result of poverty-related issues including domestic violence, addiction, unemployment, and housing issues. Currently, Manitoba's child welfare budget in 2016/2017 was $514 million, an increase of $20 million over the last four years. In 2017, the Federal Government, as a result of a Canadian Human Rights Tribunal ruling, was found to have discriminated against First Nations children by under-funding their child welfare and health services compared to non-Indigenous children in the provincially funded child welfare system. This ruling has resulted in a Federal commitment to increase spending on child welfare.

What does all of this have to do with Anna? Thirty years on, the statistics are sadly the same. In January 2018, Senator Murray Sinclair, former Chair of the Truth and Reconciliation Commission, described the child welfare system as "frozen by analysis," stating that one of the Commission's key recommendations to reform the child welfare system has yet to be accomplished. Indigenous Services Minister, Jane Phillipott, confirmed that departmental statistics verify that life expectancy for Indigenous adults is fifteen years shorter than non-Indigenous Canadians. Indigenous children are more likely to be under-educated, be victims of violence, and have more contact with the criminal justice system.

Anna is one of over a thousand Indigenous women I have encountered over my career, both as a lawyer and through my involvement with a local Indigenous women's shelter. They have shown me that in spite of often grinding poverty, they have a singular courage, born of desperation, and the resilience to rise again. Despite being faced with so many systemic obstacles, Indigenous women such as MLA Nahanni Fontaine, and Leslie Spillett, the Executive Director of *Ka Ni Kanichihk* Inc., are firmly entrenched as leaders in providing support to women dealing with domestic violence and child welfare. In addition they are providing political direction and mentorship to upcoming generations of Indigenous women.

The future health of Indigenous communities in Manitoba and throughout Canada lies with the women in these communities as the slow process of decolonization helps them to reprise their traditional roles as cultural and political leaders, as organizers, and as caregivers. Sadly, however, over a forty-year career as a practicing lawyer, I am keenly aware that there are still many more Annas out there who are alone and silent, wrapped in bruises and bruised by history.

Kaysi Fagan is a criminal defence lawyer who practices in Calgary, Alberta. She obtained her law degree in 2009 from the University of Western Ontario and thereafter obtained two Master of Laws degrees (New York University and the National University of Singapore). Kaysi formerly worked at the headquarters of the International Police (INTERPOL), is a trained firefighter, and has a black belt in Muay Thai.

Kaysi Fagan

Weeding Out the Good

I HAVE DEFENDED many prosecutions under the *Controlled Drugs and Substances Act (CDSA)*. As with anything you do long enough, patterns emerge. The usual suspect in a drug case is male, twenty- to thirty-five-years, middle class, aware of the inherent risks and sufficiently bold, reckless or dull to make the play. Less than fifteen percent of the drug clients I have defended are female, and only one percent operate alone. There is almost always a man involved and, with rare exception, the man will step up and take the heat off the woman at trial in a worst-case scenario. Contrary to the existing tide of public opinion, chivalry is not dead. In the case of Pearl Sanders, however, there was no man — she was my one percent.

Pearl, pushing seventy and grandmother of six, was a late bloomer when it came to breaking bad. She completed high school but never pursued post-secondary training or education. She embraced the so-called 'free love' movement of the

1960s and as the 1970s dawned found herself a single mother of three children receiving nominal support. Pearl ultimately succumbed to the inevitable (she married) and for the next thirty years she devoted her life to her husband. In keeping with the statistical norm, he predeceased her in 2012. She thereafter made ends meet by cleaning houses and canning peaches and other preserves which she sold to neighbours out of her kitchen.

If you had occasion to meet Pearl, you would be moved by her sincerity and kindness; she may even remind you of your own grandmother. That is, if your grandmother was charged with trafficking in half a million dollars' worth of high quality B.C. Bud ('marijuana'). In Canada, notwithstanding liberal views vis-a-vis this 'soft' drug, it is still an offence punishable by a maximum of life imprisonment.

The 'one-percent' cases tend to reveal the soul of our criminal justice system. Legal scholars often refer to the 'one-percent' as 'hard' cases — 'hard' because doing justice to a singular accused in a particular case may involve turning a century of established case law on its head; a very daunting task given the quasi-sacrosanct status afforded to legal precedent by our Courts. By way of illustration, Pearl's case raises the question, *What kind of criminal justice system would send a seventy-year-old grandmother to jail?* and yet, on the flip side, when it comes to trafficking in a half a million dollars' worth of marijuana, *What kind of justice system wouldn't?* In a hard case, the roles of Crown and defence necessarily assume heightened gravity. The answer to the two questions aforesaid and (most importantly) Pearl's fate would turn on defence counsel's ability to convince the Court of the correct nature and righteousness of her cause.

The Police Investigation and Arrest of Pearl Sanders

In August of 2014 the Calgary Drug Undercover Street Team (DUST) received a tip from a confidential informant that Pearl was transporting large quantities of marijuana from a clandestine grow operation in British Columbia to various distributors in Alberta and Saskatchewan. The tip further revealed that Pearl was renting vehicles from a company which, as it turned out, had a feature on their website that allowed public access to rental receipts with the simple entry of a driver's licence number. Using this website, the police confirmed that several vehicles rented under Pearl's name had travelled thousands of kilometres in short timeframes, which they believed was consistent with the transport of drugs. The police conducted surveillance on Pearl that corroborated the tip. They also did a 'garbage pull', finding large heat-sealed bags (typically used to transport large amounts of drugs) when they searched through Pearl's discarded trash. The police eventually obtained a tracking warrant allowing them to install an electronic device on Pearl's rental vehicle which provided the police with real-time GPS coordinates.

On September 25, 2014 the tracking device showed Pearl's low-profile rental vehicle (a maroon Town and Country van) travelling from Calgary to Salmon Arm, B.C., then just hours later heading back eastbound on the TransCanada Highway. The van was tracked by police to a gas station near Canmore, Alberta about an hour west of the Calgary city limits. Pearl was observed gassing up the van, eating a sandwich (which one observant police officer noted had 'no crusts') and then continuing towards Calgary.

At approximately 9:30 p.m. the van pulled into a Costco parking lot in northwest Calgary, where it parked beside a red Ford Focus. A man with a 'mullet' exited the Focus and spoke briefly with Pearl. The man then moved three large, heavy garbage bags from the back of the van to the trunk of the Focus. The police converged on the scene and arrested both the man with the mullet and Pearl. Police search of the vehicles revealed cash and 120 pounds of marijuana.

The police escorted Pearl down to the Major Crimes office

and endeavored to elicit a confession from her. Pearl, to her credit, kept her mouth shut. She was ultimately charged with:

> Section 5(1) of the *CDSA*: trafficking marijuana (the act of giving or transferring the bags of marijuana to the man with the mullet easily met the definition of 'trafficking' in the *CDSA*);
>
> Section 5(2) of the *CDSA*: possession of marijuana in an amount exceeding 3 kg for the purpose of trafficking;
>
> Section 354 of *The Criminal Code*: possession of proceeds of crime (i.e. money).

A police Drug Expert Report estimated that the street value of the marijuana was over half a million dollars. The expert came to the abundantly obvious conclusion that this could not possibly be a case of personal possession, because the amount of marijuana seized was theoretically enough to roll 150,334 joints. The expert opined that if a person was to smoke a joint every two hours, 24 hours a day, seven days a week that it would take her 34.5 years to smoke all the marijuana seized; that would put Pearl at close to a hundred years old. Arguing that this was personal use was not an option.

Pearl was granted bail within twenty-four hours of her arrest. My office picked up the file from there and remained at the helm for the next three and a half years. Strangely enough, the ultimate conclusion of this case came only days after I was asked to contribute to this book. It was an obvious case for me to share.

Defending Pearl Sanders

In October 2014 Pearl came to our office to meet with veteran Defence counsel, Mr. Patrick Fagan QC. I believe that no one in Canada is better at defending drug prosecutions. I say this not because he is a former RCMP undercover drug cop, nor because I have watched him win so many 'unwinnable' drug files over the years. And I certainly do not say this because I am his daughter. I say it because nobody thin-slices a file like he does. He is always willing to engage; a dogged fighter even in his thirtieth year of practice. I truly hope the proverbial apple has not fallen far from the tree.

I wish I could say that I took a special interest in Pearl's file from the beginning because of her empathetic background, the media exposure (it was reported in print, television and radio Canada-wide) or because of the size of the drug haul. But I can't. I was five-and-a-half years out of law school and I had been going flat out the entire time. Mr. C.D. Evans QC (a legal legend and beloved mentor) warned me when I was an articling student that I would leave a piece of myself in the courtroom with every case that I defended where the stakes were high. He was right, and I found myself strung-out just taking care of my own clients, let alone caring about anyone else's. With that being said, I was involved in the background on Pearl's file from the word 'go', as was my brother Sean Fagan, who had begun practicing with us earlier that year.

Within a month of Pearl retaining Patrick Fagan QC, the assigned Crown prosecutor sent over a resolution offer: enter a timely guilty plea and serve two years in a federal jail. This was accompanied by the standard ultimatum that the offer went up in smoke if the client entered a plea of 'not guilty' and that the Crown would then seek 'greater punishment' on conviction following trial.

Prior to round-filing the Crown's most generous offer of resolution, Mr. Fagan passed the file on to me for review and analysis. I synthesized the disclosure (i.e. all the information in the possession of the Crown that would be used to prosecute Pearl) and provided the following cogent legal analysis: "Looks like the police did a good job. Dead ass loser on paper, glad it's yours not mine. Good luck."

My conclusion would have led most defence counsel to seize upon the Crown's offer. But that's not how we roll. We sought instructions from Pearl, entered 'not guilty' pleas and the offer vanished. Game on. I note somewhat parenthetically that our clients often seek some sort of guarantee where they turn down a deal and roll the dice. The response that I picked up from my old man over the years is, "The only guarantee I can make is that if you plead guilty you're going to jail." This is the sage advice that Pearl received. To her credit, her instructions throughout were to burn the bridges and forge ahead. Gutsy old broad.

We scheduled a preliminary inquiry and elected to have a trial by jury. A preliminary inquiry looks just like a trial but the issue to be decided by the presiding judge is not an accused's guilt or innocence. The issue is simply this: Is there some evidence upon which a reasonable jury, properly instructed in the law, could (not would or should) convict? I will save you the suspense here — there was more than enough evidence to clear this low-threshold legal test for committal to stand trial. Often defence counsel will use the preliminary inquiry to explore weaknesses in the Crown's case. Again, I will save you the suspense — there were none here. What Mr. Fagan was able to do, however, was to convince the Crown to withdraw two of three of the charges and to only proceed to trial on a single charge of possession for the purpose of trafficking.

I believe that this agreement was a product of defence counsel's handling of an unusual situation. You see, one of the most sacred duties of the Crown Prosecutor is to protect the anonymity of a confidential informant. The fear, of course, is that compromising their anonymity will put them in danger. To that end, the Crown will redact (i.e. black out) all information that might tend to identify an informant from disclosure given to the defence. For whatever reason, that did not happen here. Mr. Fagan (in what the Court described as 'the best traditions of the Criminal Bar') simply sealed the problematic material and returned it to the Crown.

This is where the torch was passed to me and I officially became Pearl's lawyer.

Pearl attended my office to meet me for the first time in March 2016. My office is a split-level loft in a heritage building in the Beltline area of Calgary. The client waiting area sits at the bottom of a stairwell leading up to my office which is encased in partially frosted glass. As I often do, I peered down at my new client to get a feel for who I was meeting with. The first image I recall is that of her feet dangling off the edge of my waiting room chair about three inches shy of the floor. She was small, with a stooped back, short grey hair and looked every bit her age. As I walked down the stairs from my office to greet her she stood with difficulty. I could tell from her handshake that she suffered from arthritis and that the contact was painful for her. Nonetheless she grabbed my hand with both of hers and looked me in the eye as if to say, I'm yours now, take care of me. Her fear was palpable and highly contagious.

She had good reason to be afraid. Her lawyer (yours truly) was less than half her age. She was facing a lengthy jail term and she could no longer afford the services of the best of the best. The reality was that she could not afford my services either and my own previous assessment of the file (recall: dead. ass. loser.) threatened what I considered to be an increasingly positive trial record. We as a family, however, decided over lunch days prior that we needed to see this through. It was actually my brother Sean, who was turning into a more capable advocate by the day, who convinced me to take on Pearl, notwithstanding her financial limitations. His moral compass pointed (as it has since we were kids) due north.

I pause here to note that behind the scenes collaboration on files has become the norm for my father, brother, and me. Hashing out our respective challenges over steak sandwiches is one of the greatest joys of my chosen career, and it is rare for a week to go by where we don't make the time for it. The three of us are, in the words of one client, "ride or die."

During my first meeting with Pearl, I gave her my candid assessment of the challenges we faced and we discussed how (not if) to move forward. Our meeting can be distilled into five words: Keep me out of jail. While always on the lookout for an opportunity to kill this prosecution in its entirety, avoiding a jail term was the primary objective.

Pearl's trial date was scheduled for February 2017. I went back to square one with her file and noticed right away that the problematic documents that had been returned to the Crown at preliminary inquiry had yet to be disclosed in their redacted form. I sent a letter to the Crown asking that they be disclosed immediately. Months passed, additional requests were sent and all went unanswered until a few weeks before trial. The Crown would later explain to a judge that they had simply forgotten that the documents had been returned by defence. This was an honest answer and frankly, it happens. But what this created was a truncated timeline between my receipt of full disclosure and the commencement of trial. The bottom line is that I did not have sufficient time to review it and adjust my trial strategy accordingly.

In mid-February 2017, we appeared in Court to argue whether or not the trial should go ahead as scheduled. Chief Justice Neil Wittmann, as he then was, allowed me to reschedule the trial. What he declined to do, however, was rule on whether the delay of the trial caused by the adjournment fell at the feet of the Crown (for failing to provide disclosure until the last minute notwithstanding my repeated requests) or at the feet of the defence (for requesting time to prepare for trial). To me the answer was, and is still, abundantly obvious. This delay fell squarely at the feet of the Crown.

The reason that this was important is because in the summer of 2016 the Supreme Court of Canada released *R. v. Jordan,* which revisited and overhauled the test for what was considered a 'trial within a reasonable time'. The upshot of *Jordan* was that if Pearl's trial was not concluded within thirty months of her being charged (subject to subtracting any delay caused by the defence), then it was game over for the prosecution. The rescheduling of Pearl's trial had pushed the total count to forty-one months; well over the *Jordan* threshold. The question was: was the delay of the trial attributable to the defence or Crown? If it was the Crown's delay, then victory was imminent.

As the file had become somewhat complicated from a prosecutorial standpoint, it was transferred to Ms. Shelley Tkatch, a former Chief Crown Prosecutor with twenty-five years' experience. She is a disarming, hard-working, infinitely fair and capable opponent. I have never underestimated the role that she played in the outcome of this case.

A justice of the Court Queen's Bench of Alberta was appointed to hear my *Jordan* application and we proceeded to a hearing in September 2017. As Ms. Tkatch later described it, we were both, "on our 'A' game." Extensive written arguments were filed and a day was devoted to oral submissions. The issue of who caused the delay was surprisingly nuanced and complex (or so a very capable Ms. Tkatch would have the justice believe). A short time later, we received a five-minute perfunctory ruling disposing of my application with no discernible analysis of the issues. There is nothing more disheartening than to be faced with a justice presiding over a serious criminal prosecution without an adequate grasp of relevant procedural, substantive, and constitutional law. It happens all too often these days. But I digress…

One thing was abundantly clear to me after receiving the *Jordan* ruling: if I lost the trial, I had a slam dunk appeal in my back pocket. I immediately pulled Ms. Tkatch aside and candidly expressed my appellate concerns to her. Ostensibly, she acknowledged the merit of such an appeal and broached the issue of resolution.

Let me share this with you: my most basic instinct in the defence of every prosecution is to scrap it out until the last bell. Sure, this is how I was trained by my father and is to some extent a part of our shared DNA. But the raw truth is that I simply cannot stomach the thought of another human being locked in a cage because I declined to fight or could not find a way to win. I feel my losses in my bones and they become a part of me. It is the hardest part of what we do as defence lawyers. I was fully prepared to go the distance with Pearl, but the reality was that her declining health meant that she may not survive another year of legal proceedings. There was a narrow window of opportunity to keep Pearl out of jail and the decision was made to shift gears.

Over the months that followed, I provided Ms. Tkatch with medical documentation of Pearl's various conditions that showed that incarceration would cause undue hardship. Ms. Tkatch and I agreed that a conditional sentence order, often referred to as 'house arrest', would have been an appropriate penalty in these circumstances. Thanks to the Government's 'tough on crime' agenda, however, house arrest was no longer an option for most drug offences, including Pearl's. The reality was that as of November 2012, if you were convicted of drug trafficking you were going to jail — the only question was for how long.

Ultimately, Crown and defence agreed to proceed by way of a 'joint submission' (i.e. a mutually agreed-upon sentence). The plan was that Pearl would enter a guilty plea to possession of marijuana for the purpose of trafficking in exchange for a fine of $5,000 and a three-year term of probation. From my perspective, it meant zero jail time for Pearl. It would also be, according to multiple legal research databases, somewhat unprecedented.

As we were at the mercy of whether a judge would actually accept our joint submission, choosing the right judge was critical and choosing the wrong judge, fatal. I chose Judge Marlene Graham. I had appeared before her several times over the years and while she did not always decide in my favour, I found her to be learned in the law, fair, and engaged. She was rural-Alberta raised and my gut instinct was that she had lived enough to weed out the good guys (or in this case girl) from the bad. Years ago I heard her say something to the effect of "not every person who commits a crime belongs in jail." It stuck with me.

On January 25, 2018 we appeared in the Provincial Court of Alberta to determine Pearl's fate. Pearl looked colourless, no doubt as a consequence of our telephone conversation the night before when I told her to be prepared to go into custody if things did not go our way. I remember that I wore men's antiperspirant that day in full anticipation of a stressful hearing. The Crown advised Judge Graham that the typical penalty for this crime was a significant jail term. I, in turn, explained that the only way that a sentence short of jail could be imposed was if there were "exceptional circumstances"; a term which is loosely defined in the case law and rarely invoked, especially on drug files, where the primary sentencing variable is general deterrence.

Judge Graham asked the hard questions, including whether there was any case law where a fine was imposed for such a significant amount of marijuana. A resounding "no" from Ms. Tkatch and myself was followed by an uncomfortable pause from the Judge.

I tried, to best of my ability, to compel Judge Graham to feel the way I felt about Pearl. Like Atticus Finch in Harper Lee's *To Kill a Mockingbird,* I wanted everyone in that courtroom to climb into Pearl's skin and walk around in it, to understand that a jail term would not serve the best interests of justice here. I believe two things struck a chord with Judge Graham. First, both she and Pearl were from a generation where gender equality was very much an evolving concept and women grew up relying heavily on men. Judge Graham was an exception and had forged her own impressive path, but my sense was that she understood how a woman, widowed with no education or employability, could end up destitute, desperate and on the proverbial wrong side of the law.

The second thing that resonated was the degree to which Pearl's health had declined. When she was arrested with 120 pounds of a 'soft' drug, she was a lively, healthy senior citizen. By the time her sentence was rendered nearly four years later, she was crippled by pain and 'hard' pharmaceutical drugs like OxyContin pills were prescribed to her by the hundred just so she could function. As is often the case, the most damning sentence is not that which is imposed by a judge but by the irretrievable loss of a life once had. After careful consideration, Judge Graham agreed that there were exceptional circumstances and it would not be in the interests of justice to incarcerate Pearl.

Ultimately the possession of half a million dollars' worth of marijuana (enough to roll 150,334 joints) was resolved by way of our joint submission. Despite the inevitable fatigue that comes from fighting a battle for nearly four years, the irony of this is not lost on me. My sense of humour, along with my faith in the judicial system to adapt to the 'one percent' where needed, remains intact.

Reflections

While my files rarely end up in sentencing hearings, I will say this: the Government's 'Tough on Crime' agenda which, in 2012, removed from consideration the penalty of house arrest relative to most drug crimes is something that I implore future administrations to seriously reconsider. It is critical that sentencing judges be given the broadest possible latitude and discretion to address the panoply of circumstances that arise in our courts. Limiting a sentencing judge's power to ensure that justice is done and seen to be done means that in many cases, it will not be. There was justice for Pearl for no other reason than those of us on the front line would settle for nothing less; not all those accused of a crime are so lucky. Not every convicted drug trafficker belongs in a cage. Some belong in their kitchen, living out their golden years canning peaches.

Following the imposition of sentence, Pearl and I walked out of the courtroom and took a seat together. We spoke for almost an hour, and if you had overheard us you might have thought it was a conversation between a grandmother and her granddaughter. She asked me about my future plans and I surprised myself and told her the truth; that I aspired to one day have a say in drafting the law. I don't know if she told me she was proud of me or if it was just how she made me feel but I do remember her saying, "We have sure come a long way since my day."

I eventually asked her for permission to write this story, and I was stunned by how receptive she was. I fully expected her to say "no" and to assert solicitor-client privilege, as it is her right to do. Instead she lit up and looked ten years younger. She was genuinely touched that I had asked, and it struck me that perhaps no one had ever taken an interest in her life. If I didn't tell her story, perhaps no one would. For reasons I cannot explain this choked me up. It reminded me that my clients, like all people, simply want their story to be heard. It continues to be my privilege as defence counsel, to listen.

Deborah Hatch is a founding partner of Hatch McClelland Moore in Edmonton, Alberta. For nearly twenty years, she has devoted her practice to criminal trial and appellate work, appearing at all levels of Court in Alberta and at the Supreme Court of Canada. She is currently an Advocacy Adviser with the Supreme Court Advocacy Institute, and has been a guest instructor at the Intensive Advocacy Seminar and at the University of Alberta Faculty of Law.

Deborah Hatch

Shaky Foundation of Evidence

The Wendy Scott Case

THE PRACTICE of Criminal Law exposes those of us who work within it to much misery and suffering. Defence lawyers, Crown prosecutors, judges, and police officers are routinely exposed to the consequences of the worst excesses of the human condition; addiction, extreme emotion, cruelty, desperation, and neglect — both personal and systemic. Any one, or all of these things, can coalesce into events which bring individuals into contact with the system and its players.

As a defence lawyer working within the criminal justice system, one quickly becomes accustomed to misery and suffering, and while not immune to it, must learn to work effectively in the midst of it, working case by case, client by client, focusing on the legal and evidentiary issues, mindful of the vulnerability of the accused and the presumption of innocence. It is the lawyer's job to advocate for the best result, bearing in mind all of these things.

From time to time, however, there are cases which remind us of the big picture and what is truly at stake, not just for the client, but for the system, the rule of law, and our place within it as defence counsel. There are cases which remind us that systemic neglect and indifference can sometimes be overcome, and that we can surmount what seem to be insurmountable obstacles. And there are also cases which remind us that the balance in the system that makes it fair — a properly funded and independent prosecution service, defence bar, and judiciary — is at risk. Wendy Scott's case was such a case.

The Murder

Casey Armstrong, father of two adult children, lived in a small trailer in Medicine Hat, Alberta. That trailer was the scene of a violent struggle sometime during the evening of Friday, May 20, 2011, or the following day. That struggle culminated in the stabbing of Mr. Armstrong and his ultimate death. The autopsy report identified two knife wounds to his neck, either of which would have been fatal. The wounds severed his jugular vein, carotid artery, vagus nerve, esophagus, and trachea. In short, his neck was nearly severed in what can only be described as a vicious stabbing.

Curtis Harvey, a local bus driver and long-time friend of Mr. Armstrong, was the one who found him dead in the bathtub of his small trailer, on Sunday morning, May 22, 2011.

The two had been friends for years, often hanging out, drinking beers, visiting, and smoking the odd joint. On Friday morning, May 20, 2011, Harvey drove Armstrong to the drugstore to fill a prescription for some Percocet pills. Harvey testified that the Percocet was for an injury Armstrong was dealing with, and that he sometimes shared the pills with friends. After picking up the pills, the two went to the Royal Hotel Bar for a few beers, and then returned to Armstrong's trailer where they hung out together until about six p.m. Later that evening,

Armstrong made his way to Peanuts Pub, a watering hole steps away from the trailer. Armstrong was a regular there, and had a lucky night according to the pub's manager. She testified that he won some cash playing the VLT's that night. He left at roughly 11 p.m., wearing his well-worn Calgary Flames slippers, which were bound together by duct tape. What occurred between that time and the moment when he was discovered in his bathtub by Harvey, that fateful Sunday morning a day and a half later, remains a mystery.

The former manager of Peanuts Pub later testified that on that Saturday morning, she saw two thin Caucasian women outside Casey Armstrong's trailer. They were associated with an old red 'beater' car. One of the women had long, reddish hair. The woman with reddish hair put a large, dark garbage bag or duffle bag into the trunk and the women left the scene in the red vehicle.

Mr. Harvey called his friend, Casey Armstrong, several times that Saturday. There was never an answer.

The next morning, Harvey packed up some beer and went to Armstrong's trailer. It was 10 a.m. and the door was locked. He used the spare key which was kept on the porch, underneath a pillow, to enter. The television was on. He found his friend in the bathtub, wearing a blood-soaked Calgary Flames shirt and his Calgary Flames jogging pants. The bathroom was bloody.

Constable Kyle Batsel was one of two police officers who were first on scene. Batsel testified that there was blood spatter and droppings at the entrance to the small bathroom, and that the blood grew thicker past the sink. It was on the walls, and there was a substantial amount of it throughout the bathroom, as well as in the tub where Mr. Armstrong was found. A large, bloody footprint, made by either a boot or a shoe was also found within the bathroom. It appeared to be made by a work boot. Casey Armstrong was wearing moccasin-type slippers.

The Medicine Hat Police Investigators worked hard to identify the source of that bloody boot print. They sent the image to an RCMP footwear database in Ottawa to try to find a match. They went to the local Walmart and compared boot treads. They searched hundreds of Google images in earnest. They were able to determine that the print came from a size 11 men's work boot with a double E width, but little more.

Notwithstanding an exhaustive examination of the scene, no forensic evidence was located. Although it was determined that there had been no attempt to clean up or wipe down the bathroom after the murder, no fingerprints were identified, no murder weapon was found, and no DNA was located.

Charges

Two women were ultimately charged. A confidential informant told the police that Connie Oakes was responsible, and that a woman named 'Wendy' was with her. Ms. Oakes and Wendy Scott were both charged, many months later, on the basis of some of the statements made by Wendy Scott, then a twenty-eight-year-old woman who had struggled with addictions and significant mental health issues over the years. She was assessed by a court-appointed psychiatrist as having extremely diminished cognitive capacity and an IQ of 50. In spite of her struggles and challenges, her only criminal record consisted of a shoplifting charge. She had completed Grade 12 in a specialized program. She was considered by family members to have an agreeable disposition, and to always try to please others. She was also known to embellish, and to sometimes tell demonstrably false stories, sometimes for attention, and sometimes for reasons unknown.

Wendy Scott was interviewed by skilled police investigators on a number of occasions. She initially implicated three other individuals, two men and a woman, each of whom she named as having committed the murder. After providing a number of statements, she ultimately implicated Connie Oakes and later told the police that she herself was present when the killing occurred.

The three people she originally identified included 'Ginger', a woman with reddish hair who drove a red car. Ms. Scott told investigators that one of the men who committed the murder showed up at a friend's house covered in blood and looking to sell some Oxycodone pills.

On January 10, 2012, Wendy Scott was arrested and charged with obstruction as a result of one of the statements she had provided to the police. It was suggested to her that Ms. Oakes had implicated her as having committed the murder, and that investigators had forensic proof implicating Ms. Scott in the murder. Both of those suggestions were false. Wendy Scott then told the police that Connie Oakes had done it, and that she had been there when it happened. The police charged Wendy with first degree murder and conspiracy to commit murder. The charge of first degree murder carries with it a mandatory sentence, upon conviction, of life imprisonment without eligibility for parole for twenty-five years.

The Plea

Wendy Scott was detained in custody from January 2012, until she ultimately pled guilty, on a cold Alberta day that November, in the Court of Queen's Bench in Medicine Hat, Alberta. No application had been made for bail, and Ms. Scott had waived her right to a Preliminary Inquiry, a vital hearing which allows both the Crown and defence to assess the strengths or weaknesses of a case.

On November 8, 2012, Ms. Scott pled guilty to second degree murder, which, while carrying with it a sentence of life imprisonment, allows for eligibility for parole after ten years if a judge so orders. In Ms. Scott's case, both the Crown and defence asked the sentencing judge to set eligibility for parole at ten years. There was, then, some benefit to pleading guilty to the lesser offence of second degree murder. In doing so, however, Ms. Scott gave up the right to have a judge and jury determine whether the Crown could prove her involvement in the murder beyond a reasonable doubt, in a case where the only evidence against her was her own statements, conflicting and contradictory as they were. She gave up that right, signing an Agreed Statement of Facts which contained her admissions and was filed with the Court. She admitted to having accompanied Ms. Oakes, as a passenger, to Casey Armstrong's trailer between the late evening hours of May 20, 2011 and the early morning of May 21, 2011. She admitted to walking down the hallway, behind Ms. Oakes. She admitted to seeing Ms. Oakes stabbing Mr. Armstrong in the bathroom, and 'standing by' as the attack occurred. She admitted to having blood on her clothing and cleaning up when she was told to. She further admitted that "they deposited the garbage bag with the bloody clothing into a dumpster."

Also filed with the Court was a forensic assessment which had been written several months earlier by Dr. Yuri Metelitsa, a Calgary psychiatrist. That report had been ordered by the Court in order to assess Ms. Scott's fitness to stand trial and criminal responsibility. Among other things, the report noted that Ms. Scott was known to be "attention seeking at times and had the propensity to embellish stories, and would lie if she felt it would garner sympathy," that she "provided inconsistent information" during the assessment process, and that she "strongly denied involvement" in Mr. Armstrong's murder. It also stated that nursing notes indicated that she was "an unreliable historian," and that Ms. Scott denied having ever been to court, a claim which was demonstrably false. Significantly, it also contained the results of testing which had been done which indicated that Ms. Scott's "measured cognitive abilities are all within the extremely low range of ability."

When she pled guilty, Ms. Scott addressed the Court. She stated:

> My heart goes out to the family. I know I have made some bad decisions of my friends in the past and

> unfortunately, one of them, I was at the wrong place at the wrong time, and I'm very sorry. If I could do anything for the family at all, please, feel free to let me know, because I will do anything.

When the sentencing judge imposed a life sentence, he indicated that "we do need to isolate what Ms. Scott's involvement was. Clearly her role was considerably less than the role of Connie Oakes." Wendy Scott then began serving her life sentence, incarcerated first in Alberta, then in British Columbia. Ultimately, she was transferred to the Phillippe-Pinel Institute, a psychiatric institution in Montreal, Quebec.

Connie Oakes stood trial a year later in November, 2013. The Crown's entire case rested on the shaky foundation of Wendy Scott's evidence. Wendy was described by both the police and the Crown Prosecutor as having the mind of a child. Notwithstanding that observation, and in spite of the fact that there was no weapon conclusively shown to be the murder weapon, no DNA, no fingerprints, and no suspect identified as the source of the large bloody men's size 11 double E width work boot footprint, the Crown sought the conviction of Ms. Oakes. A jury deliberated for a day before finding her guilty of murder.

The Appeal Process and Legal Aid

Ms. Scott was referred to me by Lucie Joncas, a formidable, but down-to earth Montreal lawyer, who had been contacted by Kim Pate, then Director of the Canadian Association of Elizabeth Fry Societies. Lucie approached me at a meeting I attended in Montreal on a cold day in January, 2015. She asked that I consider taking on an appeal of Ms. Scott's homicide conviction — the conviction entered in 2012, when Ms. Scott pled guilty to murder. Ms. Scott was by then several years into her life sentence and was institutionalized at the Pinel Institute. She was, of course, destitute and Legal Aid Alberta had refused to cover her conviction appeal. The counsel who represented her at her sentencing hearing had advised Legal Aid Alberta that an appeal of her guilty plea "would most certainly fail."

Legal Aid is a program, in essence a fundamental social program, which serves to provide those unable to hire lawyers with coverage so that they will have legal representation in cases where vital interests are at stake. The liberty of the accused is a critical interest, and Legal Aid coverage for an individual who faces life imprisonment, whether at the trial or appeal level, is of fundamental importance if our justice system is to be fair, principled, and balanced.

The rule of law, whereby all people and institutions are subject to and accountable to law that is fairly applied and enforced, has little meaning and application in a society in which those who don't have resources cannot defend their rights. This is why many lawyers have fought to establish and maintain properly funded and independent Legal Aid programs across Canada. In the last decade especially, Legal Aid funding and coverage has declined, and the situation in some provinces, and certainly in Alberta, has become dire. It has been recognized in the last several years that the Legal Aid program in Alberta is in crisis, and that thousands of individuals who would previously have had representation by the private bar through Legal Aid are appearing before the courts unrepresented and at a profound disadvantage as a result. Through chronic underfunding and staff changes, the Legal Aid program has become excessively bureaucratic and focused on limiting coverage to accord with its lack of funding, at a high cost to many vulnerable individuals, and ultimately, to society.

After my meeting with Lucie Joncas in Montreal, I contacted Legal Aid and was advised that Ms. Scott had applied to Legal Aid in 2013 and had been denied, once Legal Aid received her former lawyer's opinion that Legal Aid coverage should not be granted.

Nonetheless, I set to work, requesting and obtaining materials over the next several months, including a transcript of her guilty plea. As I worked on the case and formulated a number of grounds of appeal, and what I thought was a fairly strong basis to seek to have the guilty plea quashed and a new trial ordered, the grounds of appeal quickly faded into obscurity as I read the transcript of the sentencing hearing. They were eclipsed by one looming issue: the facts admitted to by Wendy Scott did not establish her legal culpability for murder. I read the transcript and the agreed facts over, and over again. I waited for the essential, predictable admission: that the accused did something for the purpose of assisting the principal to commit murder. Wendy had admitted, and the Crown had accepted, that she was in the trailer when it happened, and that she was a passenger in the car which arrived at and left from the trailer. She neither provided the knife nor received it, and was not said to have done anything for the purpose of committing, aiding, or abetting the murder. I was satisfied the facts acknowledged did not meet the legal test for murder and the conviction, though based on a guilty plea, should be quashed.

I filed materials in the Court of Appeal seeking an extension of time to file the Notice of Appeal (normally any appeal must be filed within thirty days of the date of sentence, and we were more than two years out of time), and further materials to persuade the Court that there was a highly arguable appeal and that a miscarriage of justice would occur if the conviction was maintained. I repeatedly implored Legal Aid to cover Ms. Scott, who clearly was not in a position to advance or argue the appeal on her own, did not have the resources to hire counsel to do so, and was serving a sentence of life imprisonment. I sent Legal Aid numerous letters and e-mails and forwarded the materials which I filed in the Court of Appeal, detailing the basis for the appeal, Ms. Scott's cognitive challenges and financial issues, and the legal issues involved.

In September, 2015, with my motions scheduled to be heard the next month in the Court of Appeal, I received an incredible phone call from Julie Morgan, the Appellate Crown assigned to respond to my motions. I hadn't seen Julie in years as she had moved to Calgary and I practiced mainly in Edmonton and Northern Alberta. Julie and I had done many cases together over the years, and she was always well prepared, knowledgeable, diligent, and dispassionate — the kind of Crown prosecutor that defence lawyers appreciate dealing with. Julie advised me that the Crown agreed that the facts agreed to at Ms. Scott's sentencing did not support a conviction for murder, that serious error had occurred, and that she would be conceding that the conviction ought to be struck. I thanked her for her review and consideration and savoured with my colleagues the elation I felt when advised of the Crown's position. I advised Ms. Scott of this development, and needless to say, she was in a state of disbelief and was then overcome with emotion.

It occurred to me that, armed with confirmation that the Crown was conceding that the conviction ought to be struck, Legal Aid might now provide coverage, given that their position all along had been that they would not do so given that the appeal "had no merit." Being paid for the work I had done was not my main concern, but I must admit I was hopeful that I would be paid in some fashion, whether by Legal Aid or by the Attorney General. While an appropriate result for the client is what we strive for, justice for counsel includes also being properly compensated for the work which we as lawyers and our staff do in any given case. As the Supreme Court of Canada said in *R. v. Cunningham 2010 SCC 10 (CanLii)* "access to justice should not fall solely on the shoulders of the criminal defence bar..."

I forwarded Ms. Morgan's letter to Legal Aid which confirmed the Crown's position that the conviction was based on a 'serious' error and could not be maintained. Even then, remarkably, Legal Aid declined coverage and advised me that "Legal Aid would not provide coverage for work already done and that the opinions we have on file with the exception of your own have clearly indicated that they felt the appeal was without merit." I still marvel at that position, as clearly no appeal could have more demonstrated merit than one which was being won. I contacted Legal Aid yet again and spoke with the Vice President of Client Services, who indicated she would take the issue up with Ms. Suzanne Polkosnik, who was at that time the CEO of Legal Aid.

The Vice President called me back to advise that it was still Legal Aid's position that there was "no merit" to the appeal and that I was the only lawyer who felt there was. I must say that in close to twenty years of practice, I have never known the Crown to concede that a murder conviction ought to be overturned where there is no merit to the appeal. I can only conclude that the denial of coverage was for no reason other than a cost-saving to Legal Aid. It cannot be explained on any other logical basis. Inexplicably, Legal Aid granted coverage to Ms. Scott to have counsel represent her to oppose a media application to have exhibits made available to the press, while refusing to provide coverage so that she could appeal a conviction which resulted in a life sentence.

Ms. Scott's conviction was finally overturned on October 15, 2015. A new trial was ordered.

I ultimately travelled to Calgary and appeared in the Court of Appeal there to argue that the Attorney General ought to be ordered to pay pursuant to section 684 of *The Criminal Code*, a rarely used provision which I argued applied. My application to have the Attorney General pay was granted. A rate was negotiated after that appearance which was far beyond what Legal Aid would have paid, and I was ultimately compensated very properly for the work done. Justices Peter Martin, Brian O'Ferrall, and Patricia

Rowbotham marveled at the position taken by Legal Aid in the circumstances, given the seriousness of the charge, the vulnerability of Ms. Scott, and the materials which they were advised had been forwarded to Legal Aid by me, including, ultimately, the Crown's letter confirming that it was agreed that the murder conviction could not be sustained in the circumstances.

Ms. Oakes appealed her conviction and, armed with fresh evidence including Ms. Scott's repudiation of her confession and implication of Ms. Oakes, and the fact that Ms. Scott's guilty plea (relied on heavily by the Crown in Ms. Oakes' trial) had been overturned, Oakes' conviction for murder was overturned by the Court of Appeal in April, 2016. In a lengthy judgment, the Court described Wendy Scott's evidence as "exceedingly frail." The Crown stayed the charges against Ms. Oakes shortly thereafter.

The New Trial

I referred Ms. Scott to counsel in Southern Alberta (where the case was to be tried) for her re-trial. I had met Andrea Serink and Joan Blumer at the Calgary courthouse on an earlier occasion and knew them to be fierce, thorough, and patient advocates. I knew they would be well-suited to handling Wendy's case. I was pleased when they agreed to represent her. They ultimately advised the Crown that they had retained an expert in false confessions to provide an assessment of the interrogation and coercive tactics employed by the police and the propensity of those techniques to cause false confessions and false accusations, and an expert in forensic psychology to testify as to Ms. Scott's cognitive deficits. On January 13, 2017, the homicide charges faced by Ms. Scott were ultimately stayed by the Crown. Five years after being arrested, Wendy Scott was free.

Reflections

Wendy Scott's case is instructive, I think, as it highlights the failings of the Legal Aid system, the vulnerability of the accused, the ubiquitousness of wrongful convictions and miscarriages of justice and the ease with which they can occur.

In a system where so many vulnerable people depend on Legal Aid programs to protect and defend their rights, Legal Aid is in the midst of serious crisis. The liberty of many accused persons is being sacrificed while debates continue as to how and by whom Legal Aid should be funded. In the meantime, true miscarriages of justice will occur. Some will be exposed. Some will be corrected. Many will not.

Karen Hudson QC was appointed Nova Scotia Deputy Minister of Justice and Deputy Attorney General in 2016. She has practiced law in Nova Scotia for more than thirty years, serving most recently as Executive Director of Nova Scotia Legal Aid Commission, a position she held since 2009. Karen graduated from Dalhousie Law School in 1985. She and her husband, Mark Knox, QC, have two sons.

Karen Hudson

Pictures from a Lawyer's Expedition

I WENT TO LAW SCHOOL because I wanted to get a job, because I felt smart enough, and because it held a certain cachet. I was twenty-two and had never met a lawyer.

I remember the day I was accepted. I was visiting my grandmother in her small Nova Scotia village on a break from Acadia University. I was lying upstairs in the tin bed with stencilled flowers. I remember hearing her leave to collect the mail from across the street and I actually remember thinking, *I'll bet she is going to bring me a letter from Dalhousie Law School.* I hadn't been thinking much about it before that moment, but I was pretty good even back then at compartmentalizing my thoughts. I had written the Law School Admission Test (LSAT). I'd applied. The boxes were checked. I moved on.

My grandmother returned, climbed the stairs to the bedroom and said, "You have a letter." I was accepted. My journey began, more boxes to check.

In law school I studied, made good friends, met my husband, graduated, and I articled at a 'big firm'. That was what one did. It was, after all, the era of *LA Law* on television. The challenges were consuming and met because they were new. There was no particular passion that I recall. And then, in 1986, everything changed. I joined Legal Aid, and suddenly the passionate embers were lit.

A Surreal World

Back in 1986, Legal Aid was like the television show *MASH;* busy, gritty and fueled by humour, hope, and humanity.

There are many memories that I have of my years at Legal Aid in Halifax, but they are not snap shots, they are textured, living, and real. Intake day was a cavalcade of problems. A Provincial Court Judge, once described the unrelenting volume as, "The sad, the bad and the mad."

These people who frequented the Provincial, Family and Youth Court arrived in fear. The stakes were enormous, their control over events, often non-existent. You could almost hear them thinking, *Will I be released? Will I get my children back? Will I be locked up again?*

The sad outnumbered the bad, as did the mad. Mad at life, many fueled by addictions and mental illness.

My job, soon to become my vocation, was to gain their trust, perhaps offer them hope when they had little reason to give it or expect it. The memories stay with me...

Many were so very young. Johnny, as I will refer to him, was about to be sentenced and he stood beside me shaking. As the Judge begins to speak, Johnny bends over without warning and vomits in the courtroom. Or Tyrone, to pick a name, who met with me regarding a serious aggravated assault. His victim was unknown to him, the facts stark and ugly. I remember how brave he was, to really talk to me. His life was as stark and ugly as his crime. I wonder where Johnny and Tyrone are now?

The world was surreal. The young all feared going to jail. I would always remind them, "Keep your appointment with your probation officer." Then I starkly remember the day a probation officer was charged with sexual abuse of his clients. My stomach sank.

There were the women, young and old. An older client was charged with theft — theft to feed her addiction. We arrived in court armed with a plan. Progress had been made. The Crown, highlighting her long record, asked for jail. I stood and advocated hope. About fifteen minutes into my likely too-long submissions, and with a packed courtroom of cases waiting, the Judge interrupted. He pointed at me, then my client and said, "You, you may believe her," then, poking his chest, continued, "but I, I don't."

I cannot remember the exact length of the jail sentence he imposed. I do remember, vividly, being sad, maybe mad at myself as I sat in the cells with her afterwards. Remarkably, as if she was not the one in custody, she thanked me and talked about the plan and her future.

That was not the only time I wept.

I WILL CALL her Jessica. She had beautiful long red hair, a child and a pimp. The day she fatally overdosed, the justice official called me to meet at the client's apartment to retrieve her mementos, photos, and drawings for her daughter. I stood in the doorway of the small windowless bathroom, looking at the tub where Jessica's life had stopped. I remember it was a bright sunny day, but her apartment above the convenience store was very dark.

The cases of domestic abuse sucked the air out of our days. If only we had more time. I remember another young mother, with one of her young children on a busy intake day, likely looking for safety. She was fatally stabbed that night in front of her children.

One can never forget the many clients with mental illness. I felt their shame and their fear, as the facts of their lives, sometimes uncontrollable actions, and their diagnoses were laid bare for examination and dissection. Facing jail or losing their children, still for the most part, they showed up. Sometimes we could help, or even be successful. Often, we lost.

I am still amazed that more people didn't 'lose it'. I remember one who did, though. Screams from her gut shattered any calm. Chairs flew, people scattered, and the Sheriffs arrived. The Sheriffs and I took her outside the courtroom, her hands cuffed behind her. I remember putting a cigarette to her lips and stroking her hair.

The Sheriffs spoke softly to her — one patted her upper arm so gently. She was eventually released, and arrived again the next week. I saw her smile at 'her Sheriffs' standing in the courtroom and they nodded back. In my experience, the Sheriffs were the courthouse temperature takers, the eyes and ears tuned to emotions. They were professional and kind. Kindness mattered.

The years went quickly, it was a parade of poverty, with clients one day victims, the next day accused.

And yet, amazingly, they showed up, perhaps more often than anyone could expect, considering. A colleague once called it, "The constant simmer of chaos that characterized their lives."

I became Executive Director of Nova Scotia Legal Aid, Chair of the Association of Legal Aid Plans of Canada, and then Deputy Minister of Justice and Deputy Attorney General of Nova Scotia. I don't have clients anymore, but I think of them often. I have saved their cards and tokens of appreciation. On my office wall two paintings hang: one from the art gallery and one from a former client.

Sometimes I bump into former clients. Last year I was leaving the airport and someone said "Karen." I looked at her. I said her name. Twenty-five or so years had passed. She said, "Thank you." Imagine. I was her lawyer when her son was two. It was a difficult case. It turned out okay. She told me with pride that her son is now a father and so she, a proud grandmother. She reminded me of how scared she had been that whole year. She used to tell me that back then. When we were working together back then, I didn't tell her that I was also scared. For one thing, I had no right. I would go home at the end of the day. Her life could easily have gone sideways.

About three years ago, I entered into a walk-in hair salon and sat in the chair. I looked ahead into the mirror and caught the eye of the hairdresser standing behind the chair. We said each other's name at the same time. She had been a teen mom. She said, "Remember how I thought it was funny that we were both pregnant at the same time and you were older than my mother?" Her case turned out okay too. An expert had believed in her, as had the judge. After the case, she trained and worked as a hairdresser. She raised her kids as a single mom and went to university part time. She earned a degree. She was working that day; saving money before she started graduate school. Her children were grown, and she was only in her thirties. She said to me "I'm going to be earning more money than you when I finish."

What I learned at Legal Aid is that it's either a coincidence that criminal and child welfare courts are a revolving door of poverty and vulnerability, or we are doing something wrong. It's hard to believe in continuous coincidence.

What clients taught me was resilience. Resilience is fueled by hope and determination. Hope and determination make change.

Responsibility to Make Change

As Executive Director of Legal Aid, I had the responsibility to help shape change and my challenge was to offer help to more people within existing resources. Our strategic plan was shaped by listening through the chaos.

We added Social Justice Services to the menu of Criminal and Family. 'Social Justice' here means helping people with issues about income assistance, residential tenancies, Canada Pension Plan and Employment Insurance. Income and housing security can lessen intersection with the criminal justice system.

Another change was 'Criminal Duty Counsel' delivered by experienced criminal lawyers and court workers with a focus on early and final resolution. Our newly implemented 'Aboriginal Justice Strategy' included Legal Aid's first Indigenous social worker. Diversity in hiring and cultural competency training became priority focuses.

Legal Aid staff were encouraged to work with Community organizations, with the Department of Justice, with the judiciary, the law school. Change happened.

The Right Flight Plan

And then I turned fifty-five. John Lennon's song *War is Over* came to mind: "Another year over, what have you done." There was still so much to do. I applied for and was appointed Deputy Minister — another chance to help some Nova Scotians.

A Deputy Minister is like an air traffic controller: *Which planes should take off? Do they have the right flight plan and the right amount of fuel? Which planes are due to land? Where did that drone come from?*

But a Deputy Minister must also carve out time to consider new planes and new destinations in the access-to-justice journey. *Where does the criminal justice system need to be going? What needs to be better? How do we fix delays and over-representation?* I have learned that we need to continue to move away from the reactive revolving door, low tech, lawyer-centric criminal justice system.

Recently another Deputy Minister noted, "Issues can overtake strategy." In other words, it can be hard to help shape the landscape if you are always stuck whacking weeds. It is the responsibility of leaders to do the right thing — to make time for big issues, to listen to front line justice colleagues and to members of the community.

We have made progress in Nova Scotia, with a new

Domestic Violence Court, an upcoming Wellness Court in Wagmatcook First Nation, and increased diversity on our provincial court bench, including three African-Nova Scotian judges, Judge Rickcola Brinton, Judge Samuel Moreau, Judge Ronda van der Hoek, and a Mi'kmaq First Nations judge, Judge Cathy Benton.

In the past, there were no 'Wellness Court' approaches. Today our Chief Judge Pamela Williams heads the Mental Health and Opioid Treatment Court with an approach that combines offender accountability with caring. "When they stumble," she has said, "we all feel the effects."

Nova Scotia rolled out restorative justice province-wide in the adult criminal justice system in 2016. From the 2017 roundtables, we heard about the opportunity to do it even better. We brought together a governance table to make course corrections. Academics, judiciary, heads of legal aid and prosecution, victim services, Mi'kmaq Legal Support Network, and police work with the Department of Justice. Restorative Justice is a 'main thing' for Mark Furey, our Minister of Justice. It will help slow down the revolving door of criminal justice.

I emphasize 'main thing' above because it is the responsibility of leaders to listen (not be siloed) and then prioritize and accelerate change. Minister Furey often quotes change management guru Stephen Covey, "The main thing is to keep the main thing the main thing."

Sometimes I am afraid. Afraid that the right amount of time is not put on the right issues, that I am simply not wise enough or a good enough priorities juggler. But then I picture my former clients: victims, accused, offenders and parents, as they faced stark regret, confusion, anger, and fear and I think, *Buck-up. If my clients could keep going with hope, so can I. I can do something to help.*

I am shaped by conversations — with Mi'kmaq Chief

Paul Prosper, and with Professor Michelle Williams of the Indigenous Blacks & Mi'kmaq Initiative at the Schulich School of Law. I can listen to what inmates have to say and ex-offenders who are working to support the successful reintegration of other offenders. I have made time to listen to the ideas of my frontline justice colleagues.

A legal career, initially, was a box to be checked, but then I opened it. Clients and colleagues have shaped my approach — be open, be hopeful, be kind, be determined. Work hard. Keep going.

It has been many years since that lazy morning at my grandmother's house.

As I picture it now, it was like the entrance to a gallery of my life that soon carried me through the lives of so many. No longer was I able to just tick off the boxes. No longer did I want to. The law and the real people it affects, has touched and absorbed me ever since.

Barbara Jackman was called to the Bar in 1978. She is a recognized expert in Immigration, National Security, and Human Rights cases. An educator and member of many organizations she has been honoured with many awards including Honourary Doctorates from the Law Society of Ontario, University of Windsor and The University of Ottawa.

Barbara Jackman

Security Certificates

The Jaballah Case

EARLY IN MY CAREER as a lawyer, I became involved in national security cases. I had developed an interest in immigration law while I was a law student and after I was called to the bar, I set up an immigration practice with my friends, Brent Knazan and Nancy Goodman, practicing among a larger group of young lawyers who wanted to make a difference in using our newly acquired legal skills to help others. Our clients — refugees from South, then Central America — involved us in their human rights issues, life and death ones, from their respective countries. We came to realize that Canadian security officers were suspicious of the political agitation in the refugee communities in Canada and their links to movements in South and Central America — movements which may have been communist or socialist or may have supported violence against one or another of the dictatorships prevalent throughout the continent. Some of these activist refugees came under the scrutiny of Canadian security officers and so we became involved in defending them against allegations that they posed threats to Canada's security.

There certainly is a role for Canada's security service to investigate and take steps to protect Canada from security threats. However, I developed an early skepticism of 'national security' because some of my early 'clients' were actually my friends and their parents, who posed no threat to Canada. Ultimately, the ones who challenged the decision to deny them residence or citizenship were vindicated as they won their cases. But the fact that they were viewed as security risks to Canada raised serious issues for me about the right to hold and express opinions that might not be shared by the government of the day.

I have always found it difficult to reconcile government action which has the effect of supporting oppressive dictatorships, while revictimizing the refugees who sought safe haven in our country, when we hold ourselves out as a democratic country tolerant of dissenting voices. It is a highly politicized area of law, even as to who is targeted on security grounds. It is said that one person's freedom fighter is another person's terrorist. Canada differentiates on a similar basis in identifying those who are security barred. So, while I recognize that Canada must be kept safe from those who would harm us, the real issue is figuring out who that is. I do not believe it is people who engage in speech to express their political beliefs. Generally, if they are not engaging in hate speech, terrorism or other forms of illegitimate violence and are not pressing others to do so, they are not a threat to Canada.

While non-citizens targeted on security grounds are not 'criminalized' in the formal sense, they are labelled, usually as 'terrorists', and potentially face a far worse fate than criminal defendants in Canada. They face the denial of safe haven in Canada and often deportation to torture in their home countries. If not deported, they face years without lawful status — non-persons with no rights in the country. And because they are caught up in a deportation process, the safeguards which are in place in the criminal justice system do not apply. Only reasonable grounds are needed to believe the facts, not a balance of probabilities as in civil matters or proof beyond a reasonable doubt as in criminal matters. Not all of the evidence which is used against the person needs be disclosed if there are security reasons — undefined — to withhold it.

Security Certificates

It is within this context that the choice of process to secure a deportation order is significant. Removal of an inadmissible person is normally effected through a hearing before an official of the Immigration Division of the Immigration and Refugee Board. Rarely used is the security certificate process where a judge of the Federal Court with enhanced security clearance is designated to determine if a security certificate issued by the Minister of Immigration and the Minister of Public Safety and Emergency Preparedness is reasonable.

Security certificates have been reserved mostly for cases which are high profile, where the government has chosen a community leader, not just to secure that person's deportation on security grounds, but to send a message to that person's community in Canada that they should not support a particular movement. It has been used against Kurds from Turkey, stateless Palestinians, Sikhs from the Punjab, Tamils from Sri Lanka, and Arab Muslims from the Middle East.

Security certificates were first enacted in Canadian law in 1984. Prior to this there had been no formal process to challenge an adverse security finding where the government was relying on evidence that it felt it could not disclose for reasons of national security. There was no disclosure. I remember in one of my first national security cases, the security officer would not even tell my client what particular section of the Immigration Act was being used to secure a deportation order.

In 1992, security certificate cases were transferred to the Federal Court to be heard by special security cleared 'designated' judges. The process changed. Subjects of the certificates were automatically detained. Those who were permanent residents could apply for release, but not those who lacked permanent status in the country. 'Disclosure' was limited, normally consisting of nothing beyond the summary of allegations, except public articles from sources like *Janes Security and Terrorism Monitor* and the US *CIA World Factbook*. The principal part of the hearing was held in secret without the person or counsel for the person being allowed to participate. It appeared that the government's secret case was presented under affidavit from a security officer who, more often than not, was not examined by the Court. The Ministers of Public Safety and of Immigration had their counsel prosecuting the case in the secret hearing, but there was no independent counsel to the court or special advocate to test the government's case and advance the interests of the person.

I was involved over the years in challenging the fairness of this process. But it was not until 2007 that the Supreme Court of Canada accepted submissions from me and many of my colleagues, representing the three appellants and more than a dozen intervenors representing leading Canadian human rights organizations, to find that the process did not comply with constitutional standards of fairness.

Government officials responsible for drafting the new process in 1992 justified the automatic detention of all subjects of security certificates without bail on the basis that the hearings would not take long to resolve. Because immigration authorities have no suitable detention facilities, security certificate subjects were normally held in provincial maximum-security remand facilities with no access to programs or often even reading materials.

The hope for speedy hearings proved to be unrealistic. Security certificate subjects were arbitrarily detained for years at a time, and in 2007 the Supreme Court of Canada found these automatic and indefinite detentions to be unconstitutional. It also found that the hearings before the designated judges were unfair. It recognized that even where the person concerned could not participate in the hearing because the information being discussed could not be disclosed for reasons of national security, there had to be a way to ensure that the interests of the person were protected in the secret proceeding. The federal government redrafted the law. The new process came into effect in February, 2008. Hearings could still be conducted in secret in the absence of subject person, but special advocates — lawyers with experience in national security matters who were cleared to attend the secret hearings — could attend to protect and advance the interests of the person concerned in the closed hearing. This process was reviewed by the Supreme Court of Canada in 2014 and found to meet constitutional standards. Detention was no longer automatic. There had to be regular reviews of the need to detain the subject of the security certificate.

The Jaballah Case

I have represented a number of individuals from various parts of the world who were subjected to security certificates, starting in the late 1970s and continuing to the present time. Each deportation process was stressful and painful in its own way because of so many factors. The detentions were indefinite; my clients either had never been detained before and now were in maximum security or they had suffered lengthy detentions and torture in their homelands and now suffered from post-traumatic stress syndrome and were being detained for no crime — just as had happened in their own countries. The conditions of detention were awful. All faced ongoing separation from their families. All faced a threat of deportation to torture. None of them really knew what evidence the government was using to condemn them.

In this chapter, I focus on case of Mahmoud Jaballah because it continued for so many years and spanned the security certificate process established in 1992 and the new one established in 2008 after the Supreme Court of Canada struck down the laws that created the earlier process. Mr. Jaballah's case highlights both the flaws in the security certificate process and its harsh impact on the person subject to the certificate, close family members, and counsel. Few people in Canada have been subjected to such intense complex and sustained legal proceedings over such an extended period of time.

Rocco Galati first acted for Mr. Jaballah in the first and second security certificate hearings before designated judges of the Federal Court. In 2004 he withdrew from the record because he had received threats. It was at that point that I became involved in representing Mr. Jaballah, along with John Norris, who has just been recently appointed as a judge of the Federal Court. When John Norris became a special advocate in 2008, Marlys Edwardh, a well-known and highly regarded criminal defence counsel, and her associate, Adriel Weaver, an extremely competent and bright young lawyer, joined me in representing Mr. Jaballah. We continued to act for him until there was a final decision in his case in 2016.

Mr. Jaballah is an Egyptian citizen, a husband and a father of six children, and now a grandfather of more. In April, 1999 he was detained on a security certificate issued under Canada's *Immigration Act* by two Ministers, Lucienne Robillard, the Minister of Immigration, and Lawrence MacAulay, the Solicitor General. Mr. Jaballah was detained without access to bail. His wife, whose English at the time was almost non-existent, was left with their six young children — the eldest, then twelve years old and the youngest still a baby — and with limited means of supporting them.

This was the beginning of a deportation process that did not finally end until 2016, when the last of the three security certificates imposed on him was quashed by a designated national security judge of the Federal Court.

In the intervening seventeen years, Mr. Jaballah was detained for close to seven years, under house arrest for several more years after that with a requirement that he wear a GPS ankle bracelet, and subject to intrusive surveillance by Canadian border guards — so intrusive that it negatively impacted on the Jaballah children, who literally grew up with 'big brother' watching them. Mr. Jaballah remained under court ordered conditions up until the Court quashed the security certificate in 2016.

Mr. Jaballah had three security certificates issued against him. He was detained on the first one in March, 1999 until it was quashed by a designated judge of the Federal Court, in November, 1999. The Court found it unreasonable to conclude that he had engaged in terrorism or had been a member of an organization engaged in terrorism.

His freedom was short-lived: the Minister of Immigration, Elinor Caplan, and the Solicitor General, Lawrence MacAulay, imposed a second certificate in August, 2001 — just before the World Trade Centre complex collapsed on 9/11 as a result of a terrorist hijacking of passenger planes in the United States. The allegations and evidence supporting the second certificate did not differ much from the allegations and evidence relied on in the first certificate. The designated judge, found that there was some new evidence: he determined the case against Mr. Jaballah, this time finding the security certificate to be reasonable. The new evidence that the Ministers put forward included Interpol notice and fingerprints provided by Egyptian authorities who asserted that he was implicated in the supply of weapons and explosives and the escape of terrorists. Because of 9/11 there was new evidence about Al Qaeda.

The designated judge upheld the second certificate in 2003 but his judgment was overturned by the Federal Court of Appeal and the case was sent back for reconsideration. This resulted in the certificate being upheld again in October,

2006. It was quashed by operation of law on February 22, 2008, because the Supreme Court of Canada had found in three other cases that the statutory process was unfair and in breach of the principles of fundamental justice under the *Canadian Charter of Rights and Freedoms*, 1982.

A third security certificate was issued by the Minister of Immigration, Diane Finley, and the Minister of Public Safety, Stockwell Day in February, 2008. Another hearing was held under a new process established in the *Immigration and Refugee Protection Act* (IRPA) after the Supreme Court struck down the 1992 legislative process. The third certificate was quashed on June 24, 2106 by order of a designated judge of the Federal Court.

Detention and Restricted Release

Mr. Jaballah was detained in April 1999, until the first certificate was quashed in November of that year. He was detained the second time in August, 2001, and in spite of several attempts to challenge the lawfulness of his detention, he remained detained until April 2007, three months after the Supreme Court of Canada declared the mandatory detention provisions, under which he was held, to be unconstitutional. The law which the Supreme Court invalidated in February, 2007 had required that persons subject to certificates be detained without access to bail until the designated judge had either decided the certificate was not reasonable or had found it was reasonable and another 120 days had passed without the person being removed from Canada. On average it took more than two years for the judges to make decisions, and often, like in Mr. Jaballah's case it was many more years.

Mr. Jaballah's years in detention were spent in remand facilities. His last year was spent in a special detention facility on the grounds of Millhaven Institution near Kingston with other security certificate detainees. It was called 'Guantanamo North' because all of its four inmates were being held on security certificates and not for criminal wrongdoing. It was closed after the last inmate, Hassan Almrei, was released.

It is probably a mischaracterization to say that Mr. Jaballah was 'released' in April 2007 because he was put under house arrest. His wife, son, and friends became his guards, obligated to supervise and to report him if he breached any of the terms of his release. While one would expect a relaxation of conditions over time on a showing of compliance and good behavior, on Mr. Jaballah's first review in January, 2008, eight months after his release, The Justice insisted that cameras be placed around his home, because this is what she had originally wanted but it had not initially been possible to have them installed where the family was living at the time. Nothing occurred in the intervening months which justified such an intrusion into the privacy of the family, but then with hindsight, there was little to justify the other measures taken, such as house arrest or the constant surveillance by the CBSA.

As these court-imposed controls continued year after year they became oppressive, particularly in their impact on the Jaballah children. For example, for several years the eldest Jaballah child was not allowed to use a laptop computer at home while he attended university. The children could not play video or computer games that could be carried around the house. A desktop computer was allowed in the home but had to be kept in a locked room. The younger children could not access it on their own. The irony of this was that it was Mr. Jaballah's children who were computer proficient, not him. He faced no allegations of using computers for nefarious purposes. CBSA officers followed Mr. Jaballah and so if he went to a parent/teacher interview, they came too. When the children went shopping with their parents or out to dinner, CBSA officers were there watching them. As his children each became old enough to use cell phones, the CBSA acquired the right to review their phone records. It intercepted the family phone, listening in, not just to the children's conversations but to conversations between Mr. Jaballah and his counsel. We did not become aware of this breach of solicitor/client privilege until months after it had been implemented. CBSA officials claimed they did not know these calls were protected from interception.

Allegations and Evidence against Jaballah

The allegations against Mr. Jaballah were basically the same for all three certificates. He was alleged to be a danger to the security of Canada, to have engaged in subversion against the repressive Egyptian government of Hosni Mubarak, to have engaged in terrorism, and to have been a member of a terrorist and/or subversive organization. He was said to be a senior member of Al Jihad (AJ), an Egyptian terrorist organization that was alleged to have links to Osama Bin Laden (OBL).

When the first hearing started in April 1999, he was given a summary of the allegations against him, but little else. The case was grounded in his alleged associations with others and his travels. Because he was associating with others perceived to be terrorists, he was believed to be a terrorist. Because he had travelled to countries that terrorists travelled to, he was believed to be a terrorist. Mr. Jaballah contested these allegations in all three security certificate proceedings. He denied some associations and there were good reasons for contact with others. He denied being in Afghanistan, but in respect of other countries, he was a refugee with a wife and four children, trying to find a place where he could work, settle and care for his family. This is why he eventually came to Canada. The Justice in the final security certificate proceeding did not accept the 'terrorist travel pattern' theory put forward by the Ministers, finding that what some or many others may have done in travels in the mid-East in the early 1990s was not supportive of the Ministers' opinions about Mr. Jaballah's terrorist background and membership in a terrorist organization. And the Court found that the allegation that Mr. Jaballah had been in Afghanistan was not supported, given that there was no indication of when he was believed to have been there or what he may then have done there.

There were other less significant allegations, such as Mr. Jaballah acting in a way that showed he was 'security conscious'. Given that he came from a country where not being security conscious could cost him his life, it is not surprising that he may have been cautious. I have seen the same in clients from all parts of the world. They have lived a very different reality from that of most Canadians.

It was not until the third proceeding commenced in 2008 that Mr. Jaballah was given substantive disclosure of the case against him. The security service had put him and several others under surveillance and had intercepted phone conversations. For the amount of time this was going on, there was no 'smoking gun' that would have involved him in terrorist activity. The allegation was rather that he was a 'communications relay' because he had maintained contacts with some people alleged to have been involved in or associated with others involved in terrorism.

The core of the case against Mr. Jaballah was contained in the summaries disclosed in the third certificate proceeding. These were 'summaries' of parts of intercepted conversations and surveillance notes kept by security service officers. They dated back to the 1990s and had been in the government's possession and available to the designated judges in the earlier proceedings.

This chapter would be far too lengthy if I tried to cover all of the issues that arose in the course of these hearings. But there are important lessons to learned from what happened, so I have tried to focus on a few of the more important issues.

Disclosure

As noted, it was only in the third security certificate process, after 2008, that Mr. Jaballah was given substantive and individualized disclosure. This can largely be attributed to the role of the special advocates, John Norris and Paul

Cavaluzzo, both very experienced in security matters. Paul Cavaluzzo was counsel for the Arar Commission into the role that Canadian officials played in his detention and torture in Syria. John Norris has acted for many alleged terrorists in courts and before Commissions of Inquiry like the Arar Commission.

In Mr. Jaballah's case, with the disclosure that was given to us, we became aware that the security service had conducted surveillance of him and others and had intercepted some of his conversations. Rather than keep the original intercepted tapes or the officers' contemporaneous notes of surveillance, the officers had summarized their perception of the important parts of the evidence and destroyed the original notes and tapes. This formed the core of the secret evidence used to support the reasonableness of the security certificates.

This past history is highly problematic. The disclosure came only after the Supreme Court of Canada indicated that security certificate proceedings had to be conducted fairly; special advocates and disclosure were key aspects of this. For years, designated judges of the Federal Court had been convinced by counsel for the Ministers, in closed proceedings where the Minister was the only advocate, that virtually no substantive information could be released, only a truncated summary of the allegations. It did not have to be this way because the Security Intelligence Review Committee (SIRC) had been disclosing substantive evidence when it heard similar cases in the 1980s.

I thought about unanswered questions. *Were the judges simply too deferential because they were intimidated by the concept of national security? Were they afraid if they made a mistake it could result in others coming to harm?* National security is an amorphous concept peculiarly identifiable only by security officers. *Did the judges just not know enough about national security? Or did they 'buy' into the dismissive attitude shared by some members of the Federal Courts, that none of the men subject to security certificates were Canadians and so really were not entitled to fair process?*

This attitude was crystalized in the 1996 judgment of the Federal Court of Appeal in the case of Mansour Ahani. For nine years, Ahani was detained in remand facilities on a security certificate. The Court characterized his detention as unfortunate, but noted that it should be remembered that he was not being detained as a punishment. Since he was a foreign national, his detention was justified. This is one of the clearest instances of the court dehumanizing 'human rights' because those asserting them are not Canadians.

In 2004, a Justice of the Federal Court, did not see the necessity of special advocates or an *amicus curiae* in the closed hearings. That Justice indicated in one of the Harkat judgments that the Ministers had not breached their duty to make candid disclosure; the summary of allegations was adequate. That Justice then found that it was the Court's responsibility to determine the reasonableness of the certificate so that access to protected information could be limited, while balancing and protecting the rights of the person named in the certificate. This perception of their role was shared widely by other judges. However, with hindsight it is apparent that the disclosure was not adequate and the Court did not fairly balance interests or protect the rights of the named persons. It was only with the participation of special advocates in the process that meaningful disclosure was given.

In Mr. Jaballah's case, the destruction of the original notes and intercepted conversations ended up being fatal to the Ministers' case. The summaries were not sufficient. Mr. Jaballah could not compare the original intercepts in Arabic with the limited English summaries to ensure that the summary was accurate, properly translated, and complete. He could not listen to see if he could ascertain who the participants had been. There was no way to confirm the identity of the persons in the conversations. He could not test the core of the government's case against him. Because of the unfairness of this, the designated judge presiding over the proceeding refused to accept the records as part of the government's case. The core of the case was excluded, as it should have been. But it is troubling that two judges before the designated judge received this evidence without question and without disclosing it to Mr. Jaballah.

Evidence Obtained by Torture

Another part of the government's case was evidence obtained by torture. It may shock some Canadians to know that security officers do rely on evidence and information which was probably obtained by torture. It has become an important issue in recent years because of the highly publicized use of torture, not just by dictatorial regimes, but also democratic ones like the United States.

After the Supreme Court had struck down the 1992 security certificate regime, the 2008 amendments setting out the new framework contained a provision that stated that information believed on reasonable grounds to have been obtained by torture could not be considered reliable and appropriate evidence. Mr. Jaballah came from Egypt, a country known to routinely use torture, particularly against political dissidents. The issue focused on unsourced evidence, where it was not known how it was obtained by Egyptian authorities. Sometimes it was possible to conclude that torture was used, for example evidence emanating from an Egyptian trial where Amnesty International and other human rights organizations reported that the 'confessions' had been obtained through torture. But other times, the general assertions about people or organizations could not be traced to a particular torture session. Some justices adopted the reasoning that because Egypt used other means to obtain information, not just torture, it was speculation to conclude that unsourced information was obtained by torture. Nevertheless, some of the evidence was excluded.

Political Manipulation of Interpol

An Interpol Red Notice was one particular piece of evidence proffered by the government against Mr. Jaballah. It was issued in July 1999 while Mr. Jaballah's first security certificate hearing was underway. The security service said it did not become aware of it at that time. The Red Notice asserted that Mr. Jaballah was an alleged member of a terrorist organization which provided terrorists with weapons and explosives, as well as false passports enabling them to escape. It was used by the court to support his conclusion that the second security certificate was reasonable.

The Red Notice originally said Mr. Jaballah faced the death penalty in Egypt. In February 2001, our Supreme Court declared that extradition to face the death penalty was contrary to the principles of fundamental justice under the *Canadian Charter of Rights and Freedoms*. In March, 2003, the Egyptian government amended the notice to indicate that the probable penalty faced by Mr. Jaballah was hard labour for life. Then later that year, Egypt again amended the notice to state that the maximum possible penalty was life imprisonment, notwithstanding that Egyptian law continued to provide for the death penalty.

Rather than represent a *bona fide* notice in furtherance of extradition — there was no evidence of any steps taken to extradite Mr. Jaballah, although his whereabouts were well known to Canada and Egypt. Rather, Canada and Egypt intentionally used the Red Notice to support the security certificate. While one expects Canadian officials to work with foreign governments in respect of law enforcement activities, the collaboration between Canada and Egypt was of concern. Egypt was clearly targeting a political dissident and Canada was opportunistically taking advantage of this. Ultimately Marlys Edward, my co-counsel, brought the issue of the Red Notice before Interpol, asking that it be withdrawn because it was not made in good faith. Interpol withdrew it and the Court did not rely on it.

Impact of Detention and Stringent Release Conditions

Mr. Jaballah's detention over six years took its toll on him and his family. He was a survivor of torture, as was his wife, having been detained without charge in Egypt and without knowing what the government's case was against him. This was repeated in Canada, without the torture. When he was released he was put under house arrest. He had to wear a GPS bracelet. He could not be in his house without a supervisor with him. It was only after two years that he was allowed to stay at home by himself, notwithstanding that his phone was tapped, there were cameras on the doors, and the computer was in a locked room for which he did not have the key. He could not leave his house or go anywhere without a supervisor with him. The concern which led to these conditions appeared to be that he might have contact with terrorists. The case against him was based on his associations with others. However, those 'others' were not around and the court had specifically listed persons with whom he should not have contact.

Although Mr. Jaballah was always with a court-appointed supervisor — his wife, son or friends — the CBSA had officers follow him, intruding by their presence in the lives of his children. Also, CBSA officers came to give him his mail, which they had intercepted. They listened in on the family conversations and, as noted above, on calls subject to solicitor/client privilege — calls with his counsel. They had cameras watching who came in and who left. These practices infantilized Mr. Jaballah on a continual basis in front of his children.

Both the detention and the release conditions impacted on the Jaballah family. The children developed illnesses caused by stress. They were embarrassed by the surveillance. In late 2008 we challenged the CBSA surveillance of the family given that it was not contemplated in the court release order and very stringent conditions had already been imposed. I argued that the children's interests had to be considered. Two of his children testified about how the CBSA surveillance intruded into their personal lives. CBSA officers were even taking pictures of the children, and the children's friends, when they were with their father. The Justice recognized that none of the terms and conditions imposed by the Court made specific reference to the carrying out of physical surveillance by the CBSA but declined to address the issues because that Justice did not have the complete security file.

We raised the issue again before the Justice who actually had the security file and who, in March 2009 had indicated because government counsel agreed, to assume, without deciding, that the interests of Mr. Jaballah's children must be taken into account when the Court reviews the conditions of release of their father. However, that Justice went on to note that conditions could be imposed that were not in the children's best interests. In the end, the interests of the Jaballah children were not paid much heed by the Court which allowed the CBSA to continue its overt and intrusive surveillance of their father when he was with them. We had requested that they do covert surveillance. The Justice was not prepared to prohibit the CBSA from conducting overt surveillance on Mr. Jaballah when he was with his family. The only impact on the children was to annoy, anger, and frustrate them.

The impact of the detentions and the conditions of release posed the greatest difficulty for me. I watched my clients and their children, not just in the Jaballah case, but in other cases as well, become depressed or obsessive about having some control over their lives. The children grew up over the years, but they were so young initially to have to deal with the CBSA officers intruding in their lives. It shaped their childhood. The younger Jaballah children were babies when it started and young adults when it ended.

I found it easier to cope with refugees damaged by other states through detention and mistreatment, but when the injury was occurring in Canada as a result of measures imposed by Canadian officials and courts and I could do nothing as a lawyer to stop it, it impacted on me too, not just my clients. Partly this was because I did not believe the measures were needed. Mr. Jaballah's case and the cases of the other four Arab men were hyperbolized by the government and this was accepted by the Courts.

I believe it was more of matter of making a public show of taking strong measures against 'terrorists' rather then there being an actual need to impose the ridiculously stringent conditions that were imposed by the designated judges in these cases. I have represented alleged terrorists over several decades. None were detained until the detention provisions were enacted in 1992. And it was only after September 11, 2001 that the Federal Court began to impose house arrest, GPS bracelets, phone and mail interceptions and other ongoing intrusive measures, accompanied by CBSA overt surveillance. I simply do not accept that these conditions were needed for the five Arab men, but not for the Kurds, the Tamils, the Palestinians or others over the years. And the psychological and physical harm that it caused to the men and their families were not warranted. I can see the scars of long term security detentions on my clients.

Looking back now, it makes me angry, but through that time when I was so involved in the cases, I was sad. I found that I cried half the time I talked about what was happening, even when I was making submissions before the Court. For me the decade after 9/11 was painful and should not be repeated. Too many people, including too many children were unnecessarily harmed.

Lessons Learned

I believe that we can learn from what happened in Mr. Jaballah's case and the other cases. They provide a lesson in what should not be done in the name of Canada's national security, but there are no lessons as to how to avoid it. It continues in other cases to the present time.

The real lesson, as I am sure racialized communities and Indigenous peoples in Canada would recognize, is not to assume that we all share basic concepts of dignity and fairness. because we don't. I think the lesson is that we must continue to work for greater awareness of human rights and the need to have our governments promote them and the courts apply them.

Lucie Joncas obtained her Law degree in 1991 from the Université de Sherbrooke and her Masters degree in Health Law in 2001. She has been in private practice for twenty-five years mainly in the field of Criminal and Mental Health Law. Lucie was Chair of the Canadian Association of Elizabeth Fry Societies (2007-2010) and President of the Association Québecoise des avocats et Avocates de la Défense (2005-2007).

Lucie Joncas

Suicidal Clients

Recognizing the Warning Signs

I WAS CALLED TO THE BAR in the early nineties. At the time, both my parents were active in the field of criminal law in Montreal. I therefore decided to go into voluntary exile in the Eastern townships to start my own practice away from the city.

My work in Bedford, Quebec was diverse — bail hearings on Monday, family court on Wednesday, young offenders and youth protection on Thursday, and regular criminal matters on Friday. Although I refer to 'regular criminal matters', some were anything but regular. I represented individuals facing charges spanning from bestiality to the keeping of a bawdy house (not that the two were related), to failing to safeguard an opening in the ice, as well as more usual murder and voyeurism charges.

Practicing in a rural area had its advantages. I was home for dinner with my daughter every night and could keep both my skis and running shoes (or the golf clubs) in the trunk to be ready for any season.

A true camaraderie existed amongst the practitioners. On Fridays, for example, the women working in defence in the district of Bedford would get together and have lunch. We would exchange information on various subjects and discuss the decisions that had been rendered during the previous week. It was the early version of Quick Law. Bedford was, at that time, the only district in Quebec where there was an equal number of men and women working in defence.

ABOUT FIVE YEARS into my practice, on a Wednesday morning, I got a call on behalf of a woman who was hospitalized awaiting a psychiatric evaluation. The Crown prosecutor was considering laying charges of assault with a weapon, mischief, and of uttering threats. Because I was doing my Master's degree at the time with my thesis being on mental disorders, colleagues would often call on me to intervene in such files.

I therefore headed to the hospital to meet with the individual in question, knowing little about the circumstances, except for the nature of the charges.

When I arrived at the hospital, I was brought up to the psychiatric ward where a small office had been set up so that lawyers could meet with their clients privately. It was a bright room with a large window. Clients always seemed dazzled by the light when they walked in, shocked by the contrast with their dimly lit rooms. But somehow, the woman I had come to meet seemed unfazed by her surroundings.

She was petite and very pretty — well-kept, with long brown hair and hazel eyes. She hardly looked like an individual charged with aggravated assault. Her name was Ariane. In the police incident report, it was alleged that she had voluntarily driven her vehicle into her soon-to-be-ex-husband's car following a dispute.

I also understood that her eldest and youngest children both had rare conditions that required several hospitalizations. Both children had experienced respiratory failures, which required that their home be equipped with a monitor that was in permanent communication with the Saint-Justine hospital.

When I sat down with her, the first thing that Ariane mentioned was that one of her children, her youngest of three, was severely ill and needed her care. In the three or four times I went back to see her, she would plead with me to get her out so that she could get back to her children. At each meeting, I was able to reassure her that her boys had not fallen victim to any major respiratory complications, let alone failures, for several weeks. I was keeping in touch with them and they were doing well, considering the circumstances.

I told her to focus on her own health and get some rest, because as a full-time mother of three children under the age of seven, she would require a lot of energy to make up for all the anxiety. She had probably had more than her fair share of sleepless nights, given her sons' hospitalizations.

She was of the same age as me, twenty-seven years old at the time. Having gone through a separation myself when my daughter was at an early age, I could empathize with the stress and anxiety that she was experiencing. In addition, she was facing abysmal fear triggered by raising three children, two of which could go into respiratory distress at any moment.

To me, she appeared to be suffering from heartbreak and mourning the loss of her family, as she knew it. For these ills, modern medicine has not yet, unfortunately, found a treatment.

She did not, however, display the usual signs of depression or hopelessness. She went from feisty to calm and in control, as if she could voluntarily put her feelings on lock down. Every visit was different. Surprisingly to me, the treating psychiatrist conducting the assessment indicated that, "The patient is unreliable and manipulative," and that, "Information she relates as being the facts are often contrary both to what other family members report (even those she is not in conflict with) and observations by medical personnel."

Diagnosis and the Great Risks

Ariane was subsequently sent to the Philippe-Pinel Institute in Montreal to undergo a Danger Assessment. After a few weeks of observation, a clinical intervention meeting was called, to which I invited myself. It was springtime and during the two-hour drive, I was hopeful that the personnel had come to the conclusion that she no longer presented a threat to herself or others. I thought, *If she is discharged, I can even drive her back.* After all, had she pled guilty to the charges for which she had been detained, she would have completed her sentence a long time ago.

The meeting started and around the table were the psychiatrist, a criminologist, the head nurse of the treatment team, and a social worker. The only one missing was Ariane, although she was on the unit and eager to participate. They explained that some of the information that would be circulated in the meeting might be harmful to her treatment at this stage. So there I was — attending a diverse and specialized clinical assessment procedure, for the first time.

The diagnosis was pronounced: Severe personality disorder and MSBP. I understood the first part of the assessment, but in response to the confused look on my face, the psychiatrist nonetheless kindly explained MSBP. They told me that Munchausen syndrome by proxy (MSBP) was a "factitious disorder imposed on another person." The team's conclusion was to the effect that Ariane had induced the respiratory failures in her children for secondary gains and that the children were at great risk.

Their decision was made — Youth Protection Services would be called in. The team's fear was that not only was she at elevated risk of committing suicide, but she would take her children with her in order to 'protect' them. As they continued talking, I sat there, baffled!

As I drove back alone, questions lined up in my mind, like undisciplined children eagerly waiting for recess. *What did this entail? Had she lied about the child's symptoms? Did she toy with the test results to make her children appear to be ill? Could she have physically harmed her children to produce symptoms?*

Back at my office, I looked up the definition of MSBP for greater clarity. I discovered that 'Munchausen syndrome by proxy' is a mental disorder in which a caregiver makes up or causes an illness in a person under his or her care, such as a child, an elderly adult or a person who has a disability. As I understood it then, since vulnerable people can become victims, MSBP is considered a form of child abuse.

People suffering from MSBP often have poor self-esteem and cannot deal with stress or anxiety. When acting out, caregivers may get the attention they crave not only from doctors and nurses, but also from members of their community. Neighbours, for example, may try to help the family by doing chores and bringing meals.

Children who are victims of parents with MSBP can have lifelong physical and emotional problems and can even develop Munchausen syndrome themselves, as adults. Thusly, we were facing legal challenges in three different areas simultaneously — civil commitment procedures, criminal charges, and the intervention of Youth Protection authorities.

I FIRST TACKLED ARIANE'S RELEASE from civil commitment, and did so successfully. With Youth Protection involved, and protective factors in place (mother, friends, and an external medical follow up), she was free to go. The Crown agreed to withdraw the charges.

Now, we had to challenge the non-communication order against her children in Youth Protection Court. I suggested to Ariane that we should proceed carefully, and at first, concede to visits supervised by her mother.

On May 9th, the decision was rendered. Her children would not be permitted to visit accompanied solely by their grandmother. Too much had happened under Ariane's mother's watch. The visits could therefore only occur under the supervision of a Youth Protection worker.

A Peculiar Light-Heartedness

Ariane came back to the courthouse at the end of that afternoon on May 9th, at my request. I wanted to debrief on the events and plan the next steps. It was a warm May afternoon and Ariane had her hair up in a ponytail. I was concerned by her reaction to the decision after all the energy she had poured into this battle. Her light-hearted attitude surprised me. She told me she had plans with her new boyfriend. She was looking forward to the future. They were going to buy a house in the area where I lived. He had a good job working the evening shift at a large nearby computer plant and could support her. She seemed very calm and serene about the outcome and thanked me for my help. Off she went.

Her apparent serenity left me confused. In the following weeks, I tried to contact her but she wasn't picking up my calls. I figured that maybe with most of her conditions having been removed, she might have taken a trip somewhere.

I let a month go by, after which I decided to contact her mother. When I asked if she had seen Ariane lately, there was a heavy silence at the other end and I thought, *What don't I know?* What I didn't know was that on May 9th, the day of judgment, Ariane's boyfriend had found her dead in the garage. I felt a chill go through my spine. The serene and even hopeful attitude she had displayed made more sense in my mind in light of her imminent death.

Later, when I read the coroner's report, something struck me. It mentioned that her boyfriend found her at 2:00 a.m. But I knew that his regular shift usually ended at 11:00 p.m. and he would have been home by 11:10 p.m. I later found out he had stayed at work late because of a glitch and had to do some overtime. Time of death would have been around 11:00 p.m. Had this been a cry for help that had not been heard on time?

Had she relied on her boyfriend to walk in and save her, or had she really intended to end her life that day? When I called her psychiatrist, he knew about her death. The only thing he said to me was, "Be thankful she did not take the children with her."

Alive to Vulnerability

As a defence attorney, one must always be alive to the issue of a client's vulnerability in his or her interactions with the justice system. Lawyers are in a privileged position to witness the devastating impact of criminal accusations on their clients. The domino effect it triggers — loss of employment, ending of relationships, social isolation — can quickly plunge someone into a rapid downward spiral.

It is estimated that worldwide, on average, a million people each year die by suicide which in many cases is a highly preventable occurrence. In Canada alone, an average of ten people a day take their lives by suicide.

Suicide has a harmful effect on individuals, families, and the community. Statistically, it is estimated that ninety percent of the people who die by suicide were experiencing mental health issues at the time. With this knowledge, we can make a difference.

In life, I was raised with the principle that I should not ask questions if I couldn't live with the answers. In law school, I was instructed not to ask a question that I did not already know the answer to. Yet, in matters of suicidal ideation, not asking those questions can be deadly. Psychiatrists tell us that asking does not provoke or induce. In fact, it relives the person who is often submerged by suicidal thoughts but does not know who to discuss them with.

We need to ask how, when and where, if we don't later want to have to ask why? These are tough questions.

If a person has conjured up a plan, has access to a lethal means, and has set a time, those around that person need to address the issue urgently. The privileged relationship between a client and attorney can sometimes be fertile ground for this kind of reaching out to occur. Lawyers are on the front line, interacting with individuals dealing with loss and grief on various levels and of different proportions. To put it simply, we often interact with a population that is at risk.

I am not suggesting that lawyers who don't possess the appropriate skill sets should start conducting risk assessment themselves. But I am suggesting that they call upon the appropriate resources available.

TWENTY YEARS LATER, Ariane's suicide still saddens me and because of her, whenever I sense a risk, I explore it and ask the hard questions. Suicide is mostly preventable.

It has occurred, however seldom, that I have had to reach out to suicide prevention centres from my office and put my client on the line, or have to call, with my client's permission, a loved one to bring them on board. Therefore, the rule of thumb is to not to let a person with suicidal thoughts go home alone.

With a better understanding of the early warning signs, potentiating risk factors and protective elements, we, as lawyers, can be part of the suicide prevention solution. We are gatekeepers who can extend a safety net in order to prevent our clients from falling through the cracks of the system.

Susan Kyle began her legal career at the Ministry of the Attorney General as counsel in the Crown Law Office — Criminal and subsequently served as counsel to the Assistant Deputy Attorney General, Criminal Law; counsel to the Deputy Attorney General; Executive Legal Officer in the Office of the Chief Justice of the Ontario Court of Justice; and Executive Director of Justice on Target. Susan assumed the role of Assistant Deputy Attorney General of Ontario, Criminal Law Division in 2017.

Susan Kyle

Sharing Our Experiences

As Crowns, As Mothers

I AM THE FIRST WOMAN to serve as Ontario's Assistant Deputy Attorney General, Criminal Law Division — a division in which over five hundred women prosecute criminal cases in courtrooms across the province every day. Over fifty percent of the Crowns[1] in Ontario are female.

The privilege of contributing to this book, a book which gathers the voices and opinions of women in criminal law and judges from across the country, provided me with an opportunity to tell the collective stories of some of these women and what it is like to be a female prosecutor. In particular, now that my own family is grown, I have been reflecting on the early days of my career when I had a young family, and how my career choice may have impacted them. I have also been wondering whether things have changed at all in the past twenty-five years.

1 I have used "Crown" throughout this chapter. It captures Crown Attorneys, Assistant Crown Attorneys, and Crown Counsel in the Criminal Law Division.

Accordingly, the focus of this chapter will be on the experiences of Crowns who are mothers.

To prepare this chapter, I gathered a group of my female colleagues together to talk, share our experiences, and consider the impact of our work on ourselves and others. I wanted to hear how this group of experienced Crowns had built their careers within the Criminal Law Division and to learn from them.

They had a lot to tell. Much of what they had to say is relevant to anyone practising criminal law — whether defence counsel or Crowns, man or woman. We all struggle with balancing our professional and personal lives. Anyone can be affected by the darkness of the issues we see on a daily basis and the heavy workload we carry. And yet, much of our discussion was particular to women, specifically the joys and challenges of combining motherhood with a career as a Crown. All in the room had children, ranging from pre-schoolers to young adults. Many had spoken to their children about what it meant to have a Crown for a mother. Much like their mothers, those children had a lot to say.

The message I heard was consistent. Yes, the stories and facts may be different, but we collectively share a great many experiences. It was abundantly clear that we all feel exceedingly fortunate for our rewarding and fulfilling careers, despite the challenges of being Crowns and mothers. So, how do we learn from —and share — our wealth of experience? Here is a start.

Why did you choose criminal law? Why as Crowns?

I did not attend law school with the intention of practicing criminal law. Rather, I fell into what has turned out to be a more rewarding career than I could have ever imagined in any other field of law. I assumed most of my colleagues entered law school already armed with that higher sense of purpose. Not so. Roughly half of the women in the group knew that they wanted to begin their careers in criminal law as Crowns. These career Crowns were drawn to public service from the outset and remain Crowns decades later, prosecuting some of the most high-profile cases in Ontario and regularly arguing significant criminal law and policy issues before the Supreme Court of Canada. The importance of their work simply cannot be overstated.

Others stumbled into criminal law and many left the civil world, particularly Toronto's large Bay Street firms. "I needed the money after graduating law school, so I went to Bay Street for the money," said one. For others, their notions of the prestige of practising at a large private firm meant that's where they landed after law school. But they quickly learned that a civil law practice did not suit them. The more they saw of the legal world, the more they learned about the actual practice of law, the more interest they had in criminal law. Unanimously, it was the human element of the work that drew all of us to the practice of criminal law.

Interestingly, many faced critical attitudes from other lawyers when they made the shift to criminal law, and, in particular, to the Crown's office. "It must be nice working nine to five." "You're too smart to be a Crown." "You're giving up this for that?" That's a sampling of some of the comments they heard.

Then there were others who started their careers as defence lawyers, but needed to make a change when children arrived and becoming a prosecutor allowed them to stay in the field of criminal law. A single mother told us,

> My daughter was eight when I joined the Crown's office. As a defence lawyer, I would get calls in the middle of the night and I was constantly chasing clients or I would lose them. I would be making dinner and reviewing evidence — watching videos of my clients charged with impaired driving being told by police to 'keep blowing, keep blowing.'

For others, moving to the Crown's office was a preparatory move. As one former defence lawyer said,

> I knew that defence work might be trying once I had a family, and I'd heard that government work was more family friendly. And it turned out to be that way for me. I worked part time when my kids were little, and I could take off the months allocated for maternity leave.

So while long hours remain the norm for Crowns, we all agreed that working for the Crown had the privilege of benefits that are not available to our female colleagues in the defence bar and we did not need to worry about chasing clients at all hours of the night and weekends. Instead, the consistent work in a Crown's office made it a more manageable career choice for those interested in criminal law.

There was more. Defence lawyers, often sole practitioners, were attracted by the collegiality they saw in the Crown's office, particularly in large urban centres. The ability to discuss cases and, perhaps even more importantly, seek support from each other for some of the traumatic cases we were dealing with was seen as invaluable. There was always somebody to ask, "How's it going?", said one. But the talk was not always about the law and the files.

> I learned so much from my peers who were having kids around the same time as me. It's important to talk about these issues with colleagues. You can only understand if you've been there. We shared frustration, fatigue, and guilt.

Motherhood and the challenge of balancing it all

No matter which direction the conversation headed, it tended to circle back to children and the guilt associated with motherhood. Yes, there was talk about the toll their work took on relationships, and the good fortune of having a supportive spouse and other family members (their own mothers were often mentioned) but the main topic was kids. While this guilt is not unique to mothers practicing criminal law, it was universally shared.

One story was particularly telling.

> I had a big trial and I needed to get to work early every day for weeks. I would drive my daughter to the school playground and sit in the car, waiting for one other kid to show up and then I'd boot her out of the car.

There were many similar stories — taking sick kids to sit in the back of the courtroom, very late daycare pickups, missed school trips, to name a few common ones. And some pretty funny, albeit dark, ones too, involving multi-tasking and, for example, taking kids to crime scenes.

> It was the first day of a preliminary inquiry and I needed to see the scene of an armed robbery. So, on the way to Rosh Hashanah dinner that night, I put the girls in the car and headed off to the scene to re-enact the crime.

A balanced life, it was agreed, is not possible with children in the mix. "We can never feel we are the best lawyer, the best mother, the best spouse. It's coming to that acceptance." All had conducted long, multi-week trials, during which their heads were down. They barely saw their children. When they did, they felt guilty about the darkness they were bringing into their homes, and their inability to fully engage with their children, so immersed were they in their cases.

"Guilt," as one said, "is the worst advisor." It's possible to dismiss that emotion, however, everyone understood intellectually that guilt was the price of admission, but emotionally… that is another thing altogether.

Getting a handle on guilt

Well into their child-rearing years, how had these women contextualized and compartmentalized their guilt? They had answers. First, many hadn't fully anticipated the challenge of combining motherhood with prosecuting criminal cases. Some had been very young when they launched their prosecutorial careers ("I was naïve. I hadn't thought about family at all.") Others, assured of their ability to handle any situation, assumed adding a couple of children into the mix would be easy. Said one, "I had *no* concept of how exhausting it would be." Another added, "I never thought I would be cleaning my kid's vomit and then giving submissions to a jury thirty minutes later."

Given the often coincidental timing of starting a career and becoming a mother — some were north of thirty — was difficult for some. Recalled one,

> I was learning to be a lawyer and a mom at the same time. It was hard enough to carry a case load - and everything takes so long at the beginning. I found it really rough.

Still others had watched female colleagues confidently combine motherhood with career and who made it look easy — they hadn't thought that, maybe inside, these women were working very hard to give off those "calm vibes." That was tough in a different way — thinking they might not be measuring up in those early days of lawyering and mothering.

Most had ultimately accepted the idea that being a "good enough" mother is actually good enough. As one said,

> I had my child later in my career. I'd been working on child abuse cases. It was more than full-time hours and I didn't have any work-life balance before my daughter was born. After her birth, I went back to child abuse cases and felt anxious about working with those issues and the hours I was putting in. But it was like riding a bike, I knew how to do those cases and I had to let a lot of stuff go. Being 'good enough' is the best advice, but it's hard since we're all perfectionists.

All acknowledged that wrestling with guilt was difficult

to do on one's own. And social pressures didn't help matters. One spoke about her child who was experiencing some health challenges. The professionals she went to suggested maybe she should be taking some time off from a job she loved. But when she and her child finally landed with a specialist doctor, she was advised to keep working. She was told,

> You need to have a life independent of your child and he needs to have a life without you...and he's completely fine and amazing. Don't quit your job.

The right words at the right time helped alleviate the guilt.

The conversation wound back to the support offered by work colleagues, especially those who also served as mentors. One name came up repeatedly — Sarah Welch. A long-time Toronto Crown, she died of cancer in March 2018 at the age of sixty-six. She had served as a mentor for several in the room. For many, now in mid-career, Sarah was a trailblazer. She joined the Crown's office at a time when far fewer women had that opportunity. Said one,

> With [Sarah] as my mentor, it meant that I didn't experience any type of discrimination. There was never a 'you're not equal' moment.

Another of our group noted that,

> It was Sarah who sat at the back of the courtroom and made sure judges treated us right. She would not put up with her Crowns, male or female, being yelled at by a judge. She made a difference.

During Sarah's time as a Crown, all agreed, the advancement of women was noticeable. And, all agreed, they were in the debt of women like Sarah.

Being part of a team has its ups and downs. First, not all Crowns, particularly in remote regions, have the luxury of walking back to the office and commiserating with a fellow Crown. Second, not all collegiality was exactly positive.

Offices and those in them can develop a culture that is not supportive of those with family obligations.

> My unit is a macho environment. I wish people would not be scared to be seen as weak because they have family responsibilities. In many ways, you're not quite tough enough if you have to go home to look after kids.

Then there are the pressures of handling criminal files – which sometimes boils over.

> There were times when I'd tell my co-workers, 'I didn't leave the apocalypse of my home to come into the office to hear you jackasses arguing.'

Often what was shared tipped into deep black-gallows humour.

> I decided to change files from a particularly dark one. I picked up a bail file only to find a man charged with the murder of his best friend. According to the notes, he'd eaten the friend after he'd murdered him.

At times like these, "that's where collegiality comes in," with the ability to talk with another who's walking the same path and, as a result, can bring things back into focus.

"We need to be able to rely on one another as Crowns," recognizing that prosecuting is, simply, an inherently difficult profession.

> We are the shock absorbers in the courtroom. We have to keep it together when judges, witnesses, police officers, and others are freaking out. We work in a trauma centre. When we leave the courtroom, we need people to talk to about what we do. And those people are your colleagues. You can't talk about your work outside the office and you certainly don't want to take it home to the dinner table.

But, work and its pressures have myriad ways of seeping out of the office.

She sees things differently...

There was also another side to this parenting ledger. Many of the adult children spoke about learning to argue [from their Crown moms]. "She had a miraculous ability to shut down any argument. It was very impressive, but quite frustrating." Sure it had been frustrating when they were younger but now? "I am grateful for that argumentative trait. I am able to make my opinion heard, despite being a quiet person myself."

> Was I paranoid as a kid? *So* paranoid. When other kids were getting the freedom to walk around the neighbourhood alone, my mother was always telling me: 'Be careful of this, be careful of that.' I think I will be a completely paranoid parent. The worry genes run deep in our family.

Another chimed in,

> My mother had an intention to put an idea in our minds that there are bad things in the world that could lead towards a dark future of possible crime. I have always thought that because of her job she sees things differently than other parents do.

Yet another reminded her Crown mom that, "I hesitated to talk to you about injustices at school, because you would elevate it."

Our adult children have a more sophisticated take on what it is to, as my own son puts it, "be the kid of a Crown." When he was young, he recalls,

> I didn't have the context of not being the kid of a Crown. You were my mom and I didn't think to compare myself to my friends who didn't have mothers working as criminal lawyers.

What adult children now see and are able to assess, younger ones take for granted. As it was time for Crown moms to weigh back in we heard

> Our problem is that, as Crowns, we know too much. We're hyper-sensitized to the dangers in the world. We know what's out there. I often don't know how to balance that. The world isn't so scary, yet my five-year-old is terrified. I know too much. Now she knows too much.

There was much talk about safety: not allowing children to go into public bathrooms on their own; creating family 'safe words' — just in case; elaborate discussions about the concept of consent ("if you want tea one day, you may not want it the next…"); not allowing children to play with guns and violent video games; tremendous fear of children learning to drive ("every car could be driven by a drunk driver"); and many, many ways of learning to be wary of strangers and saying "no."

"We had a friend come over to our house. His arm was in a cast. My six-year-old son asked him if he'd been shot." A graphic reminder to this mother that the effects of her work were coming home with her and being absorbed by her children, despite her best efforts to keep them off the dinner table.

There were stories of over-the-top parental panic when a child didn't turn up at home at the prescribed time. And then there were the text conversations with kids. One went something like this:

> Mom: Where are you?
> Daughter: Home.
> Mom: Your phone is allegedly at the Eaton Centre. What did you buy?
> Daughter: Nothing.
> Mom: Honestly, come home, there are awful people at the Eaton Centre who will pull you into a life of prostitution. You think I'm joking?
> Daughter: I know you're not joking. LOL.

The issue of parental overcompensation loomed large. People worried about those long trials when they disappeared from their children's lives for seven or eight weeks. "I was in Grade 6," a now-eighteen-year-old recalled,

> I had a huge social studies report due and my mom edited it seven times until she finally let me hand it in. My mom got the best mark in the class and my mom always over-compensated.

That tendency to over-compensate at home further exhausts an already over-worked group of Crowns.

All were concerned about the impact their mothering skills, particularly their anxieties, were having on their children both now and in the future. The mothers of adult children were able to provide some comfort to those of younger ones. But that comfort had its limits — "I don't think I brought my work home, but my children have developed a very dark sense of humour, which they attribute to me." One adult child said,

> Watching someone invest so much of their time into something that from the outside looks dauntingly academic intimidated me. I wanted to get away from it… I would tell her, 'I never want to work as much as you do.'

That inside view of the justice system developed a variety of traits in these children — knowledge, understanding and empathy, to name three.

Learning about the justice system from their parents gave them an understanding of it. One said,

> I know that a challenge to the law actually strengthens it. Most of my friends, for example, hate any defence lawyers who defend sexual predators. I understand the purpose of the work of both Crowns and defence lawyers.

But it's not just the justice system, it's the broader concept of public service that these adult children see as valuable and essential to a well-functioning society.

> Having a mother in the public service sector was a reminder that she was a vital contributor to a progressive, safe and fair society.

My son expressed the same attitude,

> Your work provided me with a level of respect for our institutions and the rule of law. It's put a high value for me on civil service. If you had been a Bay Street lawyer, I would not have had the same understanding of the social contract.

Another added, "Her views coloured her world and surely shaped mine."

The understanding these young people have has led to empathy for those less fortunate.

> My mother has empathy. You might expect the opposite given her role as a Crown, but she sees that everyone is human and that often the crimes people commit are a by-product of their harsh upbringings.

Comments like that arose repeatedly throughout our discussion. *How did they come by that empathy? How was it instilled?* Some of it, the mothers agreed, came from simple osmosis — the fact that their kids "are exposed to a lot more than most kids." For others, conversations with their children focused specifically on the nuances of society. People who do bad things, for example, are not often bad themselves. Sometimes it came from a less intentional place. One Crown recalled,

> My kids were complaining about me not going to their soccer practices. I was working on child abuse cases in those days, spending time with kids who have the worst lives. I told my kids they were lucky there was food in the fridge and that I didn't beat them.

We are privileged

With that empathy came the realization, amongst the older children, that they had a privileged upbringing and that solid start had served as a good launching pad into adulthood. Like their mothers, they had a good understanding that with privilege comes responsibility. "To whom much is given, much is required."

The practice of criminal law takes a toll on those who practice it. Whether you are a young Crown or an experienced one, whether you are a man or a woman, or whether you have family responsibilities, the job performed by every Crown is challenging and integral to the proper functioning of our criminal justice system. I learned from my colleagues at our recent gathering, and later called "our group therapy session" that there are common experiences shared by Crowns who are moms. We struggle to find balance, we fear bringing darkness into the lives of our children, and we over-protect them as a result of the constant exposure we have to the victimization of children and others. On the other hand, we find ourselves reassured in the shared discovery that our children are both more resilient and observant than we had thought.

Despite the different paths to becoming a Crown, prosecutors dedicate themselves, day in and day out, to serving the public in a meaningful and substantive way as vigorous advocates and quasi ministers of justice. Without exception, and despite the many challenges we face in our illusory quest for balance, each of us feels enormously fortunate and fulfilled in our professional lives. We are also assured that our children have benefited from their mothers' commitment to justice and will continue to benefit as they forge their own paths ahead. [2]

2 Thank you to Susan Lightstone for her tremendous assistance in putting together this chapter.

Jill R. Presser was called to the Ontario Bar in 1997. Her practice is devoted to criminal defence, with a focus on criminal appeals. She regularly appears at courts at all levels, defending clients facing charges involving serious violent crime, drug offences, white collar offences, and domestic assaults. Jill teaches, writes and speaks on a variety of topics in relation to criminal law, evidence, mental health, law and technology and women in the legal profession.

Jill R. Presser

Mom's *Rea*

Motherhood, Criminal Defence, and Guilt

I REPRESENTED Joshua Dowholis, an HIV-positive gay man in his criminal conviction appeals to the Court of Appeal for Ontario. Josh had been convicted of three counts of aggravated sexual assault and two counts of forcible confinement. He had met the four complainants, also gay men, at a bathhouse in Toronto where they had smoked crystal meth together. They then went back to Josh's home where the incidents of sexual assault and forcible confinement were said to have occurred.

At trial, one of the complainants admitted perjury on a number of points in his testimony. All of the complainants were among the most inconsistent, self-contradicting and confused witnesses I have ever encountered. This was, by no means, a strong Crown case.

Josh Dowholis maintained his innocence. Based on the trial transcript I read and the man I came to know him to be, I believed him. And yet, the jury convicted Joshua Dowholis.

Blatant Homophobia

One of the jurors made blatantly homophobic jokes in a public forum while Mr Dowholis' trial was ongoing.

After the jury rendered its verdict convicting Mr Dowholis, but before sentencing, trial counsel discovered that the jury foreman had discussed the case on live radio. This juror was the producer and one of the on-air personalities for a popular Toronto shock-jock radio show. While acting as jury foreman, once before conviction and a few times after, he went on the radio and made homophobic jokes about Mr Dowholis, the complainants, the evidence, and homosexuals in general:

> He expressed disgust at their [Dowholis and the complainants] behaviour and lifestyles, particularly their sexual practices, drug use and promiscuity.... The tone and content of the conversations reveal prejudicial attitudes towards the lifestyles of some gay men.[1]

Trial counsel brought audio recordings and transcripts of the radio broadcasts to the trial court. She asked the trial judge to re-open the conviction on the basis of fairness, taking the position that the convictions could not stand if they were the product of homophobic bias, or the appearance of such bias, in the jury. But the trial judge refused to re-open the trial or investigate whether there was actual or apparent juror homophobic bias. She ruled that she was unable to act because it was a jury that had rendered the verdict, and the jury was by this time long disbanded. The trial judge made the radio broadcast tapes and transcripts into exhibits and left the matter of homophobic bias for the Court of Appeal to decide.

I REPRESENTED Joshua Dowholis in the Court of Appeal. When I met him, he was already well into his penitentiary sentence.

1 *R v Dowholis*, 2016 ONCA 801 per Benotto JA (for the majority), at paras 25 - 29.

I inherited the appeal and had to start from the beginning with it, causing delays.

I came to know Joshua Dowholis as a gentle, polite, patient, and soft-spoken person. I liked him as a person and as a client. I believed he was factually innocent and wrongly convicted.

I cared about him and his appeal. I cared about the impact of homophobia on fairness in the justice system. I wanted justice and vindication for Joshua Dowholis, and, by extension, for the LGBTQ+ community in Canada.

But for me, this was not just a progressive person's thirst for justice for a historically disadvantaged group, although it was that too. For me, this case was not just about trying to help my client, but also, this case was personal. I cared about battling homophobia and seeking justice for LGBTQ+ Canadians because I am the mother of a queer daughter.

I wanted to win the Dowholis appeal for Joshua Dowholis, for all LGBTQ+ Canadians, and for my own child.

As a woman, a wife, a mother and a criminal defence lawyer, I often have competing demands on my time and attention. Two weeks before the Dowholis appeal was scheduled to be heard in the Court of Appeal, I wanted to lay in and start preparing heavily. Around the same time, my daughter's first relationship ended. She was devastated.

Naturally, my daughter turned to her mother for consolation. She looked to me for maternal words of wisdom and comfort, for my welcoming shoulder and open arms. Above all, she looked to me for my time and attention.

I wanted to be there for her. But I also needed to prepare for the Dowholis appeal, which I felt on some levels, was also for her.

How could I prepare for my appeal and mother my hurting child properly at the same time? I struggled with massive pangs of guilt.

Mommy Guilt

All criminal lawyers are intimately familiar with guilt. The criminal justice system turns on whether our clients' criminal guilt has been proven beyond a reasonable doubt or not. Our professional lives are all about trying to show that it has not.

But for criminal defence lawyers who are mothers, guilt has a whole other meaning too. Working mothers experience 'mommy guilt', gnawing painful pangs over the hours spent away from our children while at work.[2] And while all working moms may experience mommy guilt, those of us who are mothers and working criminal defence lawyers may have reason for especially acute guilt.

In its 2008 study into the retention of women in private practice in Ontario, the Law Society of Upper Canada concluded that there is a real problem with retaining women in private practice. They noted the 'unique challenges' faced by women criminal defence lawyers, but left those particular challenges for further study in the future.[3]

That future study happened, in 2016, when the Criminal Lawyers' Association published the results of its study of the retention of women in the criminal bar. It concluded that women experience unique gender-based challenges in the practice of criminal law, which appear to lead to women leaving the private practice of criminal law at higher rates than men. The majority of survey respondents

> ...viewed the unpredictability of work hours, unpredictability of income, and the difficulties of having and raising children while working in criminal law as

2 Julie Bort, Aviva Pflock, Devra Penner, *Mommy Guilt*, 2005, Amacom, 2005 at p. 137. See also, Harriet Lerner, *The Mother Dance*, 1998 Harper Collins at p. 75, "One thing you will learn on the job is guilt. You may feel guilty about leaving your children for your work and guilty about leaving your work for your children. You will no doubt also feel guilty about feeling guilty."

3 Law Society of Upper Canada, *Final Report – Retention of Women in Private Practice Working Group* (May 22, 2008), at paras 1-3 and 280.

> probable reasons why women may choose to leave the private practice of criminal law. [4]

The practice of criminal defence is challenging. The hours are brutal and unpredictable. The work is stressful and adversarial. The economics, especially for those of us who take Legal Aid Certificates (as so many of us do), are incompatible with family life. Legal Aid's inadequate hourly rates and tariffs mean we have to do a high volume of work in order to make a living wage. These challenges, inherent in the private practice of criminal defence, make it hard to do the job, make a living, and still have enough time to raise children. This is why we have a problem retaining women in our bar. It becomes very difficult to stay when you are a mom. And, if we do stay in the practice, the guilt we experience when we choose our clients' needs over those of our children, whether out of financial necessity or not, is ferocious.

As criminal defence lawyers, our clients have much on the line — liberty, reputation, career, and family. Their needs and our responsibilities to them can be overwhelming. *How do we represent our clients fearlessly and zealously and still have enough time and energy to meaningfully mother our children? How do we balance the extreme needs of our clients with the every day needs of our own children?*

The fact that I have a supportive spouse who is the father of my children has not solved these challenges. To be sure, having a partner who supports my career and co-parents makes this all easier. But like so many mothers, I have been the primary caregiver. My kids look to me first, and lean on me hardest.

So I am no stranger to mommy guilt. In fact, it has been my constant companion and fellow traveller.

---

4 Natasha S. Madon and Anthony Doob, "The Retention of Women in the Private Practice of Criminal Law: Research Report," Criminal Lawyers' Association, March 2016 at pp. 7 – 9; 11-13.

When I first returned to full-time practice, after having taken time out of my practice to be at home with my daughters, my younger daughter was not quite three years old. I will never forget how much it hurt me when she threw her arms around my legs and implored me not to leave the house for court. "Don't Doe,[5] Mama! Don't Doe!" Or the time when she was five years old and I missed most of a parents' open house at Sunday Hebrew school because I had been outside in the hallway dealing with an arrest call. When I finally made it into the classroom, all the other children were sitting with at least one parent, happily engaged. My daughter was sitting alone, dejectedly staring down at a piece of paper that she was folding and unfolding in her little hands. She looked so sad. When I attempted cheer and asked her what she was holding, she told me that everyone was writing prayers with their parents. She had to write hers alone. I asked her to show me her prayer and could barely hold back tears when I saw this in my daughter's shaky child's printing: "Dear God, Can you please make my mama not work so hard? I miss her."

There was the time when I was in Ottawa the night before a case at the Supreme Court of Canada. My mother had to take one of my daughters to the hospital emergency room by ambulance. Of course I knew my daughter was in the best hands possible, and she was ultimately fine, but how to deal with the worry over distance? How to perform in high stakes litigation with so much worry about one's child? How to reach through the phone lines to reassure the child enough or send her enough love and care to see her through the medical emergency?

Then there was the time when I was working at home of an evening (a common enough occurrence). My older daughter stuck her head into my home office and told me that she was considering committing a crime, because at least that way she'd be assured of getting my time and attention. Or the time I

5 Her slightly speech impaired not-quite-three-year-old way of telling me not to go.

overheard her talking to a friend who had a stay-at-home mom, saying, "No, my mom never volunteers for class trips or to come into the class, cause she's always working. I don't even ask her anymore."

Constant Struggle

I have constantly engaged in the struggle-to-juggle, careening between the needs of the children and the needs of the practice (to say nothing of the needs of my spouse or my own needs). And always, *always* feeling like I was letting someone down. [6]

For my part, I do see the upsides of being a working mother. Needless to say, there is the income (albeit less than what lawyers of equal experience in other areas of practice earn). There is also the psychic benefit of doing challenging and interesting work. And, I love being able to set an example for my daughters of trying to use one's education, experience and energy to help others. I believe that being a criminal defence lawyer is a way to do good in the world. As criminal defence lawyers, we get to help real people, often very vulnerable and marginalized ones, often facing the absolute worst moment of their lives. I stand beside them and behind them as they face the machinery

6 Sharon Hays, *The Cultural Contradictions of Motherhood* cited in Susan Maushart, *The Mask of Motherhood: How Becoming a Mother Changes Everything and Why We Pretend It Doesn't*, Penguin 1999 at p. 208: ". . . .if a mother works too hard at her job or career, some will accuse her of neglecting the kids. If she does not work hard enough, some will surely place her on the 'mommy track' and her career advancement will be permanently slowed by the claim that her commitment to her children interferes with her workplace efficiency. And if she stays home with her children, some will call her unproductive and useless. A woman, in other words, can never fully do it right."

See also, from Maushart, at pp. 122-123: "Today's prevailing cultural mythology tells us, in the pithy language we reserve for bumper stickers and commercial sloganeering, 'Girls Can Do Anything!' Maybe so, but the stubborn and politically incorrect fact remains that we cannot do everything. And more specifically, we cannot mother young children at the same time as we pursue a life of our own devising, or at least not in the way we have been encouraged to devise it. . . . We find, most of us, that our most heroic efforts to remain in charge and on top of things are as nothing compared to the juggernaut of a young child's needs. The fact is, once a woman becomes a mother, her life will never again be quite her own, or in quite the same way. It's something few of us want to believe, let alone discuss, let alone – dare I say it? – to celebrate. But it remains, nevertheless, the single defining feature of a woman's life on the far side of the great divide."

of the state. I help them resist the disproportionately weighty resources available to the prosecution, which can deprive them of their liberty, their reputation, and sometimes even their family, their work, or their ability to stay in this country. This work is incredibly important to the maintenance of democracy and the rule of law, and it is important too to the people we are trying to help. In doing this work, I know that I am showing my daughters, by example, that win or lose, they too must try to help others. That they must try to make their lives matter.

But important and beneficial as it may be for a mother to work outside the home, the daily struggle-to-juggle is real. Mother guilt is real and painful.

Keeping Balls in the Air

In the waning days before I had to argue the Dowholis appeal, I was particularly torn. I needed to be engaging in concentrated heavy preparation for an appeal I believed to be important in the interests of justice, for a client I believed to be innocent, and for all LGBTQ+ Canadians, including my own daughter. At the same time, I needed to be consoling that daughter and helping tend her broken heart.

I did not know how to keep all of these balls in the air. So I did what I do in these situations, what I think all of us do — I frenetically ran scrabbling from one priority to the other and back again, attending neither to my satisfaction, highly anxious about both. It was an endless loop of 1. Scamper frantically; 2. Prep for appeal; 3. Scamper frantically; 4. Comfort child; 5. Repeat. All other priorities (including, for example, the other daughter, the children's father, sleeping, eating, and so on), were pitched overboard in a reckless attempt at triage. My daughter's repeated mantra, "I'm fine ma, go do your work" offered no solace whatever, because I knew it was not true or sincere. Besides, I wanted to be with her to hold her hand and offer encouragement. I also wanted to win the appeal.

Inevitably, the date for the hearing of the appeal arrived. We argued it and, ultimately, thankfully, won. The majority of the Court[7] allowed the appeal, holding that the conduct of the jury foreman created a reasonable apprehension of bias. They held that the juror's on-air derogatory comments about the participants in the trial and about the trial process, as well as the failure of trial safeguards (for example, the juror's oath and the trial judge's exhortation not to discuss the evidence or the jury's deliberations with others) would lead a reasonable person to perceive that the juror would not decide the case fairly.[8] Importantly, the majority of the Court also recognized that homophobia is as corrosive and unacceptable in the justice system as other kinds of prejudice, like racism.

The decision of the majority of the Court represented a step forward for the LGBTQ+ community in its search for justice in Canada.

There was vindication for Joshua Dowholis too. The Court unanimously allowed the appeal and ordered a new trial. The Crown ultimately decided not to reprosecute.[9]

Less definitively, but certainly over time, my daughter survived and overcame her first love lost. In fact, she is thriving.

I will always wonder about the ways I could have done (and still could do) things as a mother and a criminal defence lawyer differently, better. *Been a better mother? Been more*

7 *Dowholis, supra*. The majority of the Court, Benotto and Tulloch JJA, allowed the appeal on the basis of reasonable apprehension of bias. Doherty JA concurred in the result but would have allowed the appeal on a different basis.

8 *Dowholis, supra*, per Benotto JA, at paras 1, 2, 25.

9 The Crown's stated reason for deciding not to reprosecute Mr Dowholis was that it would be in the public interest to do so because he had already served his whole sentence. My own view, having read the trial transcript, is that the Crown could not at all have been confident of a reasonable prospect of conviction on a retrial given the perjury and inconsistencies of the Crown witnesses at the first trial.

present? Loved harder, or less distractedly?[10] But on the morning of the Dowholis appeal, my lovelorn daughter left me no reason to question. She handed me the following note

> Dear Mama
>
> Good luck in court today, and every other day.
>
> I know you are working to make this country a more just place. I'm proud of you and hope to do something as meaningful with my life as you've done with yours.
>
> I love you.
>
> XOXO

I put that note in the pocket of my court robes and it is there with me always in court, to this day. I carry the pain and the joy of motherhood with me into the courtroom, and the pain and the joy of the courtroom into mothering. For better or worse, this has been my children's experience of being mothered. I hope they will say it has been mostly for the better.

---

10 I am constantly reminded of the brilliant poem, "This Be The Verse" by Philip Larkin

They fuck you up, your mum and dad
They may not mean to, but they do.
They fill you with the faults they had
And add some extra, just for you.

Rosellen Sullivan graduated from University of Ottawa in Criminology and from Dalhousie Law School. She was Junior Inquiry Counsel to Commissioner Antonio Lamer at the Lamer Inquiry which examined three wrongful convictions in Newfoundland and Labrador. She now practices criminal law with SBK Defence in St. John's, regularly appear in all levels of court in the province and has appeared at the Supreme Court of Canada.

Rosellen Sullivan

Youthful Innocence Lost

When I was initially asked to (forced to) consider writing a chapter for this book, I was reluctant. What could I add to this series? How could I compliment such amazing women. I threw my hat in the ring under the generic topic of a unique criminal case in Newfoundland and Labrador. I considered writing the story of my very first, and still favorite, criminal trial. In Newfoundland, it is considered a comedy. It wouldn't have translated well. That can be a story for another day.

In fact, the case I've chosen to write about is not a comedy, nor is it unique to Newfoundland and Labrador. It is similar, I'm sure, to ones that play out every day in Canada. It is not a wrongful conviction. Nobody went to jail. Nobody died. A boy who was charged with an offense was found not guilty of that offence. Yet, so many lives were ruined.

I am struck by the reality that, regardless of the fact of being innocent of an offence, truth can do nothing to reclaim innocence, youthful innocence.

I am a criminal defence lawyer. A one trick pony. I love my job. Much of my practice involves defending people accused of sexual assaults and Internet-based sex offenses. It is part of my every day. I lose absolutely no sleep over it. That's not to say, I don't lose a lot of sleep over the actual defence; I lose a lot of sleep over that. But my clients and the charges cause me no ethical conundrums whatsoever. Of course, I'm not holding a placard in support of sexual predators. I am, however, holding a placard in support of the *Canadian Charter of Rights*. I consider the most important part of my job to hold the law enforcement agencies to the most important part of theirs: to abide by the rule of law and to abide by the Charter.

Still, a lot of my clients are guilty as charged. This is a fact that does not, in anyway, affect how I do my job. I put forward the best possible defence, ethically, and professionally, in accordance with the law.

When I have a truly legally, factually, and morally innocent client, I lose sleep.

When I have a truly legally, factually, morally innocent thirteen-year-old client, I lose years.

Thirteen-Year-Old Client

A few years ago, I get a referral from another lawyer who is the friend of a dad in need. The friend's thirteen-year-old son is being investigated for sexual assault against a six-year-old girl.

"No problem. I can represent him. Thanks for the referral. Much appreciated." I write the appointment in my book and I go on about my business.

Then, I meet said thirteen-year-old.

I meet my client, and his parents. He is catatonic. They are hysterical. They are going to be a problem.

"My kid would never…."

"He's such a good kid…"

I hear the same comments from every single parent of every single youth, of every single male under thirty I've ever represented. Of course, my initial reaction is, *Of course, mom, he's the perfect child. I know he doesn't leave the house. I know he's in his bedroom twenty hours a day. I know....*

But I see a boy. Not a thirteen-year-old 'almost man'. No 'almost stach'. No ball cap with a giant bib that I want to slap off his head to the corner of my office. A boy. A little boy. He looks to me to be about eleven, say twelve, conservatively. He is a baby. He is, at best estimates, eighty pounds. I know he weighs less than my giant eighty-six pound dog.

His parents are beside themselves. They cry. He doesn't. They tell me the allegation. Their son, my client, is charged with sexually assaulting a six-year-old girl. The families know each other. As usual, in smaller communities in Newfoundland, everyone knows everyone.

I assure them that this is what I do. I can help. Yet, I know full well the outcome doesn't matter, the damage is done. Full stop.

We arrange for him to be charged at my office. The officer is totally respectful. She speaks directly to his thirteen-year-old face. She is a professional. So is he. His parents cry.

I learn, over time, that he is withdrawn by nature. Anxious at the best of times. Adores his older brother. Excels at sports. He, actually, is a good kid. He doesn't cause trouble at home. He doesn't cause trouble at school. He plays video games, street hockey, collects recyclables, walks the dog.

I learn, very quickly, that what I had perceived as a lack of emotion is a complete and deliberate act on his part in order to save his mother from actually dying of fear and heartbreak. I know that he knows that as soon as he shows emotion his mother will disintegrate and he will never forgive himself for that. As is often the case with young people charged with offences, he now has the added stress of having to protect his mother and the added guilt of feeling responsible for what he perceives is ruining his family. He becomes the parent overnight.

I get disclosure. My heart breaks. For everyone.

We have the first court appearance within a month. I ask for a closed court. I insist on the earliest possible trial date. Over the summer? Between Grade 8 and 9? So this doesn't fuck him up too much. Everyone agrees. Let's not fuck him up too much.

And this is the how it comes to be that my innocent client loses his innocence.

A Six-Year-Old Complainant

The complainant's mother has three children. Her husband, as is the case with many Newfoundlanders, works out of province for three weeks a month. The six-year-old complainant is the oldest child. She has a younger sibling who is in day care. One day, a note comes home from daycare after an incident of "inappropriate behaviour" amongst the children at daycare *(I'll show you mine if you show me yours)*. While the complainant's mother talks to the younger sibling about this behind closed doors, the six-year-old complainant sits outside the bedroom door crying. She wants in. Her mom tells her that she needs to talk to her sibling about inappropriate touching, and that this doesn't concern her.

"I was touched." she said.

"What!, By Who"?

"By Johnny." *(Not his real name.)*

The mom, of course, doesn't know what to do with this information. She, of course, comforts her child and, over the course of several hours, asks very direct questions. The mom, of course, has no training in how to professionally interview a child. There are, of course, many leading questions. The allegations start off vague, but over the course of the next couple of hours, and in response to the leading questions, get more specific. Horrifically detailed, in fact. I don't blame the mom for this. She isn't aware that the power of suggestions is exponentially multiplied when coupled with the positive reinforcement of undivided attention.

She is a mom who thinks her child has been harmed. Everyone I know would have done the same thing.

I immediately retain a psychologist who trained the police in taking statements. This included training on how to avoid leading questions and how to properly extract reliable evidence from a child witness. The goal of such training is to avoid contamination of the witness's initial disclosure. I have used this expert witness on several occasions because he trained the police.

The six-year-old is seen by a pediatrician. In the presence of the complainant, the doctor is told of the allegations. During the course of the examination, the doctor notes a tear in the hymen but says the examination is "normal." The doctor ultimately concludes that there is nothing in her observation that "could substantiate the allegations or be of assistance to a prosecution."

The mother also contacts the police. She gives a statement about the disclosure. The young complainant also gives a statement recounting the details of the alleged offence. She is energetic, articulate, and sweet. She plays with a stuffed animal provided by the plain clothes officer who uses her first name. She looks comfortable and, frankly, unfazed. She tells the officer what she had told her mother. She describes his penis. Well, she describes 'a' penis. She describes, vaguely, where it happened in the house and where everyone else was. These details change over time and it is hard to tell from the statement whether she is talking about one or multiple incidents. She is inconsistent about times, sequence and details, but she is six years old. As I say, she is asked, and describes, what my client's penis looks like.

The Pediatrician's Medical

I am aware that there has been a pediatrician's medical exam because the visit to the doctor is documented in the file. Also, there is a 'consent to release medical information'. There is no report. The existence of a report is disclosed to the Crown and defence on the Friday before the trial, which was meant to commence on Monday. The report itself is disclosed on the Monday, the first day of trial.

I read the report and think the conclusion renders the report completely irrelevant. I ask the Crown to proceed to trial, despite the late disclosure. Despite not having the medical information, and having no plan to call the doctor, the Crown changes its trial strategy. The Crown notifies me that they want to call the doctor as an expert witness. A postponement is granted. In response to the Crown calling the pediatrician, I retain an out-of-province expert, in anticipation of arguing that the doctor's evidence is inadmissible because it is irrelevant. Because the results are within "normal" range, it will not further the Crown's case. An application for costs is filed, due to the late disclosure and the seemingly random decision of the Crown to rely on the doctor even though it is not part of the Crown's initial case.

Postponed Until After the School Year

In the meantime, the trial is postponed until the school year ends. I reiterate my objection that the doctor is not qualified to give the opinion the Crown wants to elicit, which, in any event, I argue, was irrelevant. A "normal" examination, I object, does nothing to further the Crown's case, it is probative of nothing.

Have you ever asked a thirteen year old, in the presence of his parents, to describe his penis? I have. I consider this a low point in my life, let alone my career. I ask this of my young client knowing with a hundred percent certainty that if a male lawyer asked me to describe my vagina in the presence of my parents, or even not, I would grab his perfectly engraved letter opener and stab myself in the jugular, right there, in his office.

But, the complainant described a penis. She described it in such a way that I couldn't ignore. I know this is potentially going to be important. So, I have to tell a thirteen-year-old boy two things: "I need you to go to a doctor to have your penis measured," and "I need you to take a picture of your penis for me, please."

I have actually asked these things of adult males. A penis gets described. A picture can contradict that description. I'm okay with that. I have never asked this of a child. I think, briefly, that perhaps I am doing far more damage than the actual complaint. But I immediately know, in the face of the long term consequences, that this might be a necessary evil.

I assure the boy that I will never look at the picture unless it becomes a hundred percent necessary. Also, I have to consider the Child Pornography legislation. Satisfying myself that this will be protected under s.163.1(6)(a), I calmly ask my client's dad if he could take a picture of his thirteen-year-old son's penis, save it on a USB drive, bring it to me, and delete the original picture. I wonder, *Is this the right thing to do?* But what I do know is that if there is a potential issue with the description given by the complainant, it may well be important. I can't let my mind wander to what my thirteen-year-old self would have done if this humiliation was compounded by a judge, in a court, having to look at a picture of my genitals.

We go to trial within nine months of the charge, but four months after the original trial date was derailed by the medical report. In the meantime, my client's family still lives in the same community as the complainant, as his parents are unable to sell their house. The children cannot help but see each other. Each time they bump into one other, the mothers quickly usher their respective child in an opposite direction — except for the one time, when the complainant is jumping on a trampoline chanting, "Johnny's going to jail, Johnny's going to jail." I don't imagine this idea came to her on her own. She says it with a rhythmic levity that is completely incongruous with the content.

My client stops eating because he can't keep food down.

He goes from 'small' for his age to what I would consider dangerously underweight. He calls home frequently from school, asking to be picked up. He avoids his friends and his parents. He rarely leaves the house. He withdraws from life. He is stressed by the charges, of course, but he is also consumed by the impact this is having on his family. He wears it like he used to wear the jersey of his favorite hockey team.

The trial starts with the evidence of the officer, the mother and then the complainant.

The officer's evidence is uneventful. She testifies to the time and circumstances of the disclosure and the statement of the mother and complainant.

The mother outlines the circumstances of the disclosure. It becomes very obvious, very quickly that the complainant was vying for her mother's attention and was upset to have been left out of the discussion with her sibling. The mother confirms that the disclosure immediately followed the mother telling her that she needed to talk to her sibling about inappropriate touching and that this discussion did not concern her. She readily acknowledges that she probably asked very direct, leading questions.

The complainant testifies via CCTV from another room. She is, again, sweet, and comfortable. But she describes the allegations very differently from those she described in her statement. She says things she has never said before. She says things that could not have happened. On cross examination, I ask, "Did you watch the video of your statement?" "Yes," she says, she did." She watched it with her mom.

I also ask if she remembers the things she described in her statement happening? "No," she says. But she remembers that she said those things in her statement. "Yes," she remembers when mommy told the doctor what happened. "Yes," she remembers when mommy told nanny what happened, and again when mommy told daddy. What is strikingly obvious is that she is irreparably influenced by the leading questions she has been asked and repeatedly being exposed to the adults in her life talking about the allegations. She has no recollection of any of these things actually happening.

While she testifies, again she plays with a stuffed animal. Again, as she had been in her videotaped statement, she is bright, articulate, and unfazed. I ask her if she is going to get a prize after she "did a good job today"? "Yes, I'm going to the candy store." Is she just saying what she thinks I want to hear so she can go to the candy store? "Yes".

What the fuck am I doing? How did we get here?

After she testifies, I ask the Crown its intention, given her testimony. My expert has not yet arrived in the province and I can head him off at the pass. The Crown intends to call the doctor. My expert arrives as planned.

On the morning the doctor is to testify, the Crown approaches me to tell me the doctor does not feel qualified to give the opinion the Crown wants her to give. "Good," I said, "that makes two of us." I was invited to meet with the doctor who reiterated this to me and my expert.

Again, I ask the Crown's intention. I am advised the Crown intends to proceed but will not call the doctor as an expert, rather she will be called as a witness of fact. She will testify about her observations of nothing. I will cross examine her about her observations of nothing.

I have an expert sitting next to me at the tune of several dollars a second. Reminiscent of the *Loony Toons* cartoon when everything looks, to the hungry wolf, like a cooked turkey, every time I look at my expert he is a cartoon dollar sign.

Still, we continue. The doctor testifies about her observations. Yes, her observations are of a "normal" exam; an exam that could not further the Crown's position in any way. The doctor readily accepted this on cross examination. I do not call my cartoon-dollar-sign expert.

The defence calls no evidence. My client is acquitted.

In Retrospect

In the circumstances, if my thirteen-year-old client had been an adult, I would have closed the books, celebrated the success and moved on. I don't think I would have given it another thought.

But my client wasn't an adult. He was a child who had been thrown into the adult world. He was forced to pole vault over every single normal teenage experience a person could ever have. I doubt he will ever have a normal intimate experience that isn't tainted by this experience.

He is still withdrawn, more so, if that is even possible. He trusts no one. In fact, he doesn't even have the comfort of the soft parental pillow. In his mind, he has completely destroyed that. He's "used up" all his parents' love. He doesn't yet understand the concept of unconditional love. And it doesn't matter anyway, he will never accept it.

As his lawyer, I've probably done hundreds of trials since his. My practice has not changed all that much. But I think of him often. Most recently I thought of him when his mom called me. He applied for a job at a fast food restaurant. He was rejected because his records check was flagged. While I have since been assured by the police that this should not have happened, this is cold comfort to my clients. At the ripe old age of sixteen, he has been branded a sex offender.

Jennifer Trehearne BA (McGill), LLB (Osgoode), clerked at the Court of Appeal for Ontario and the Supreme Court of Israel. Upon her call to the Bar, she practiced criminal law as an associate at Schreck and Greene, appearing in all levels of Court in Ontario. After serving as counsel in the Office of the Chief Justice of the Superior Court of Justice, she returned to the practice of criminal law as a sole practitioner.

Jennifer Trehearne

Another Day in Court

A Eulogy

This is Wonderland

In February of 2005 I had been a lawyer for just over four months. In law school, I had declined all opportunities to engage in real casework, afraid that I lacked the required knowledge to do a good job, and apparently convinced that this knowledge would somehow be magically bestowed upon me by the end of law school. For my articles, I accepted an excellent opportunity to clerk (to work for judges), a position that allowed me to learn by watching great litigators at work, but did not involve conducting litigation. And so, when I was called to the Bar in the fall of 2004, I found myself like a licensed dentist who had never looked into a real mouth.

Nonetheless, I managed to secure a position as an associate for two highly respected lawyers (now Justices Andras Schreck and Mara Greene). They were everything I wanted to be — smart, kind, and committed to providing society's most marginalized with the best legal defence. Thus, with a dawning horror that I really had no idea what I was doing, I set out to do my best for them and for their clients.

In my new capacity as associate, I was often sent to appear at Toronto's Old City Hall. Old City Hall is a stunning Richardsonian Romanesque structure in the heart of downtown and as I was relatively new to Toronto, its stained-glass windows and mosaic floors gave me a quiet thrill. Indeed, my grandparents had photographed Old City Hall during WW II when my grandfather was sent 'down East' (as Toronto is known to Westerners) for his wartime service. As Toronto's red streetcars passed by on Queen Street, I was proud finally to pursue what I wanted to make my life's work. I felt as though I were living in an episode of *This is Wonderland*, a CBC sitcom debuting at the time about a young female defence lawyer in Toronto.

Like my fictional counterpart, I soon discovered that Old City Hall's attendees encompass every stratum of our society. Handcuffed prisoners in orange jumpsuits and blue shoelace-less shoes are herded past eminent judges and lawyers in the hallway. The beauty of the building is paralleled only by the stench of the prisoner cells on a hot day. The worried relatives of the accused sit on benches outside of courtrooms, crying. The children of the incarcerated are brought to court to catch a glimpse of their parents. Homeless people, charged with the criminal offences that beleaguer the poor, wander the halls.

Tucked in the back basement corner of the building is courtroom 102, a specialized mental health Court. The courtroom program is meant to provide some form of specialized justice to some of our society's most marginalized. Accused wearing tin foil hats or other objects meant to ward off demons pace the halls outside the courtroom, often ranting to themselves. Harried lawyers, frequently in ill-fitting suits that reflect a focus on the well-being of their clients to their own self-neglect, rush in and out. Mental health workers with the patience of saints stand at the ready to assist, never judging.

The Human Being, My Client

It was in 102 Court that I was asked to appear in February of 2005 for a client of the firm. For the purpose of this recounting of events I will call him Michael Johnson, although that is not his real name. I obscure his identity so that I can be candid in the details of this story without violating solicitor-client privilege, and also out of respect for him, as I cannot now ask him whether I may invoke his story.

When I met Mr. Johnson in February of 2005, he had been homeless for eleven years. He suffered from schizophrenia, refused to take his medication, and was floridly psychotic. He was a tall, thin man with dark wild hair. He rocked forward and backward, and was given to explosive outbursts. His clothes were torn and dirty, and his shoes did not match. He believed he could assassinate the Prime Minister through prayer, and that he could cause earthquakes with his mind. But what dominated his thoughts was his conviction that he was being eaten from the inside by aliens. He picked and scratched at his face as if to remove them. I had never met anyone so deep in the throes of mental illness. His pain was palpable.

Mr. Johnson had a criminal record relating to an assault with a weapon and criminal harassment. He was given a term of probation for these offences which required, among other things, that he attend at a psychiatrist's office as directed by his Probation Officer. He had subsequently been arrested again and charged with a new count of assault with a weapon, and was released on bail. Mr. Johnson now found himself again in custody for having refused to see his psychiatrist as his Probation Officer required. He was being held in courtroom 102 for a bail hearing. My task was to secure his re-release on bail.

Defence lawyers do not get good publicity in mainstream media. We are often depicted as greedy and underhanded. But even positive depictions of defence lawyers usually focus on our work in Court, skillfully and dispassionately cross-examining witnesses. And, depictions of defence lawyers, whether positive or negative, are almost always of middle-aged men in expensive suits. What the public does not understand is all the background work good defence lawyers quietly do before a matter even comes to Court. In the case of representing the mentally ill, the public does not see the lawyers, many of them young, and many of them women, sitting in the dirty hallway of the basement of Old City Hall or other similar courthouses, armed with a copy of *The Criminal Code* and a cell phone, calling homeless shelters and other community resources to put together a viable plan for their clients. The public does not know that these lawyers are paid by Legal Aid for only a fraction of their time. And yet that is the truth about much of the practice of criminal law.

Indeed, in Mr. Johnson's case, the prosecutor's initial position at the bail hearing was that she would consent to Mr. Johnson's release on bail if I could line up supervision in the community for him. And so, I found myself sitting in that basement hallway, trying to put together a release plan for my client. He was estranged from his family and had nobody to bail him out. The bail program (a program that acts as surety for accused persons with no family or friends to assist with bail) was unwilling to work with Mr. Johnson, as he had previously refused to cooperate with them. Mr. Johnson's conviction for assault with a weapon related to a shelter worker, so local community services were reluctant to assist. But with some begging and pleading on my part, a local homeless shelter worker agreed to accept Mr. Johnson to his shelter if released. He even agreed to work with Mr. Johnson to ensure he saw a psychiatrist available to the residents of the shelter, and to remind him of his court dates. That shelter worker, and others like him, are some of the unsung heroes of our society.

Making those arrangements took the whole day, so Mr. Johnson's matter was adjourned to the following day to deal with bail. I returned to my office on a dark, wintry evening.

The following day, a different prosecutor was present in Court. He took a position different from the first, indicating that even with the release plan I had arranged, he would not consent to Mr. Johnson's release. Having gathered that the first prosecutor would return the following day, and wishing to benefit from her position, I adjourned Mr. Johnson's bail hearing again.

On the third day, the first prosecutor had returned. However, she, too, had changed her position. Now her consent to Mr. Johnson's release hinged not only on a release plan, but also a determination by the psychiatrist in Court that day that Mr. Johnson was fit to stand trial. Mr. Johnson had now been in jail for three days. The time was taking its toll on him. His cheeks had begun to bleed where he was picking at them. He was increasingly agitated.

The Blunt Instrument of Criminal Law

An accused person is unfit to stand trial if, on account of mental disorder, he is unable to conduct a defence or instruct counsel. In particular, the question is whether the accused can understand the nature or object of the proceedings, understand the possible consequences of the proceedings, and communicate with counsel. To be fit, an accused need not act in what others perceive to be his or her best interest. An accused is entitled to his own defence, and to present it as he chooses. Thus, the question is whether the accused has sufficient mental fitness to participate in the proceedings in a meaningful way.

Accordingly, the reality is that while everyone else in the courtroom may look at an accused person and think he should clearly be in hospital, if that accused person is fit to stand trial it is his prerogative to instruct his lawyer to pursue bail so that he may be released back into the community. Further, if an accused is fit to stand trial, then it is outside the power of the judge to send the accused to the hospital against his will; the judge must choose between the community and detention in a provincial detention centre.

In Ontario, our provincial jails are all maximum-security institutions, with little meaningful programming for prisoners. They are often dirty and overcrowded. Prisoners with mental health issues are often the target of violence by other prisoners. Specialized psychiatric care is largely unavailable.

In Mr. Johnson's case, I believed him clearly to be fit to stand trial. As long as I remained calm in my discussions with him, and re-focussed him on the issues at hand, he was able to understand the court process and to instruct me. The fact that he believed he could cause earthquakes with his mind did not impede his ability to understand the role of the various courtroom participants, the nature of the charges he faced, and the choices available to him. I therefore obtained his instructions that he was willing to demonstrate his fitness to the psychiatrist present, in order to secure the prosecutor's consent to his release on bail. I was so sure that Mr. Johnson was fit that I did not perceive there to be a real risk in this course of action. I was obliged to take his instructions to pursue bail.

To my surprise, the psychiatrist who assessed Mr. Johnson in the courtroom claimed that in his view there was, perhaps, an issue of fitness. Thus, the prosecutor did not consent to Mr. Johnson's bail, and instead we entered into a hearing to determine whether there was, in fact, an issue of fitness. When called to testify, the psychiatrist conceded Mr. Johnson understood the courtroom process. However, he said he thought Mr. Johnson might have difficulty communicating with counsel. When I asked the psychiatrist whether he found it surprising that I had been able to obtain Mr. Johnson's instructions to subject himself to the very assessment for fitness which was now the topic of dispute, he could only say that he was unaware of that fact. And he could not explain in any way why he thought Mr. Johnson might have difficulty communicating with counsel.

I do not know why the psychiatrist suggested Mr. Johnson might be unfit. I remain of the view that there was no issue of fitness. Based on what happened next, it appears the psychiatrist had concerns about the prospect of Mr. Johnson being released on bail, and so I speculate that perhaps he raised the issue of fitness with a view to Mr. Johnson's detention in hospital rather than in jail. In any event, whatever his motivation, having been forced to concede that he had no real basis for suspecting Mr. Johnson to be unfit, he added that in his opinion, Mr. Johnson as dangerous. He described Mr. Johnson was angry, and said that if he got frustrated with someone, he might take retaliatory action.

Whether Mr. Johnson might be dangerous was outside the scope of the opinion the psychiatrist had been called to proffer. It was improper for him to venture that opinion. It was irrelevant to whether Mr. Johnson was fit to stand trial. But if Mr. Johnson's fate had not effectively been sealed already, it was at that moment.

Having heard the evidence of the psychiatrist, the judge ruled that there was no issue of unfitness. Thus, we turned to the merits of bail, with the question being whether Mr. Johnson should be detained in jail or released into the community. And as I made my arguments on the issue of bail, I began to realize that although I had won the battle, I was likely going to lose the war. I was correct that Mr. Johnson had no history of failing to attend court, nor any proven history of failing to comply with court orders. But I was asking the judge to release back into the community someone with a violent history, an outstanding charge of violence, and a severe mental illness that remained entirely untreated. Mr. Johnson had previously assaulted a shelter worker, and I was asking that Mr. Johnson be released to a shelter. If the judge needed any more encouragement to detain Mr. Johnson, he had just been told by a well-respected psychiatrist that Mr. Johnson was prone to violence. There was little else I could have done to cobble together a release plan for Mr. Johnson in short order, but I realized that the plan I had been able to put together was entirely unsatisfactory.

As I made my submissions on bail, the judge put these very concerns to me, and it became clearer to me by the moment that Mr. Johnson would be detained. I started to picture Mr. Johnson in jail. I could not believe that we, as a society, would send Mr. Johnson, whose behavior was clearly dictated by his mental illness, to a place where we sent others for punishment. I looked at him sitting in the prisoner's box, hoping for his release and trying to control his agitation. His vulnerability in a jail setting was overwhelming. I imagined him subject to strip searches and other significant impositions while consumed by his paranoia. I imagined him trying to cope in the face of violence perpetrated by prisoners much stronger than he. It was like punishing someone for having cancer. It broke my heart.

I knew why Mr. Johnson was angry. I was angry for him. I was angry that he had lived on the streets for more than a decade. I was angry that he had slipped through the cracks so many times that now he found himself in an impossible position. I was angry that there were insufficient resources even now to address his situation in a meaningful way. I was angry that no matter whether he won or lost his bail hearing, things would likely not get better for him. I was angry that his anger was being used as a justification for his own detention.

And at the same time, although I had been following Mr. Johnson's instructions as I was required to do, I was concerned that somehow by doing so I had played a part that would result in his incarceration. I wondered whether the hospital would not in fact have been the best place for Mr. Johnson, and whether I had somehow done him harm by contesting the issue of fitness.

At that point, I had been weighed down for four months by the feeling that while my work was of fundamental importance, I did not know what I was doing. It was my third day of watching Mr. Johnson descend further into mental illness. I did not make it through my submissions before the tears began. The clerk of the Court passed me a Kleenex box and a note that said "don't be scared, you're doing great." I finished my submissions and sat down. Bail was denied.

After the bail hearing, I went to see Mr. Johnson in the cells to explain to him that he had been denied bail. Despite my best efforts, I was still wiping away tears. At that moment, poor and sick Mr. Johnson stopped scratching his bleeding face, looked at me through the glass, and asked, "Why are you crying?" Embarrassed, I told him I was not crying, but simply had a bad cold. There was a pause as he studied me. Then Mr. Johnson, floridly psychotic, said something I will never forget, "No, I know you're crying. But it's okay. At least I know one person cares about me."

What Seemed the Inevitable

That bail hearing was the last time I saw Mr. Johnson. I appeared for him a number times thereafter in an effort to move his matter forward to secure his quick release, but he was never brought to Court. Each time I was informed he was in the hospital for a medical issue.

When he was not brought to Court in April of 2005, however, there was no explanation forthcoming. I left the courtroom and went to the lawyers' lounge. Sitting on the couch of that crowded and too hot room overlooking the courtyard at Old City Hall, I called the jail to find out the reason for Mr. Johnson's absence so that I could explain it to the Court. The person on the other end of the phone simply told me that Mr. Johnson had died. He said it with a casualness that made me think I had misheard. There was no further explanation. When I went back to the office and described what had happened, a colleague asked me if I was okay. More than anything, I could not get over the feeling that somehow I had known all along that this was going to happen.

Mr. Johnson died in custody on April 2, 2005. To this day,

I do not know how he died. He was not an old man. I asked about the cause of his death, but was told those details would be released only to his next of kin. I tried to find his family, but he had a common last name and the task proved impossible. As far as I know, his death went essentially unnoticed, with no inquiry into its cause.

Looking Back and Moving Forward

For many years, I looked back on that bail hearing with embarrassment. I would criticize myself for failing to control my emotions, for being unable to be clinical in my assessment of the case. I also continued to feel that I had somehow let Mr. Johnson down.

All these years later, I have learned to forgive myself, if only a little, for having become so upset. I can look back with some compassion at the me who was doing her best in an untenable situation. More importantly, I have learned to look back on that day as an ongoing source of strength in my continuing career.

Even the most mundane of days in criminal courtrooms, as my appearance for Mr. Johnson must have felt to everyone else (apart from Mr. Johnson), has significant consequences. Mr. Johnson's liberty was at stake. The denial of his liberty no doubt took even more of a toll on him than it does on an accused who does not struggle with mental health issues. A charge of breaching probation is about as run-of-the-mill as it gets in the criminal courts, and yet the consequences for Mr. Johnson were dire. I knew that so clearly at the time. It's easy to forget that as the years go by and appearing in Court has become routine. But it is crucial to remember.

I do not know what the answer is when someone's mental illness causes them to pose a danger to the community. I understand why we strive to respect the integrity of the accused to conduct his defence as he sees fit. I also understand, better in retrospect, why the judge was reluctant to release Mr. Johnson on bail. I understand that he was caught between a rock and a hard place. But I believe as a society we can do better. As I felt so keenly at the time, we need to provide meaningful resources to those in Mr. Johnson's position even before they are arrested. And following arrest, we need more resources for defence lawyers to call upon, and we need there to be better choices available for judges to make. Those with severe mental illness struggle to cope in our jail system. Their psychiatric symptoms are not only difficult to treat in that setting, but are exacerbated by it. Their suffering is compounded.

It is easy to become cavalier about injustices if injustices are the norm, much easier than it is to care about them. But one of the great values of defence counsel in our democracy is to continue to identify, and rail against, those injustices.

INDEX

Books in the Durvile 'True Cases' Legal Series

Tough Crimes: True Cases by Top Canadian Criminal Lawyers
By Edward L. Greenspan *et al*
Book 1 in the True Cases Series

Edited by C.D. Evans & Lorene Shyba

"Tough Crimes demonstrates that Crown prosecutors and criminal defence lawyers do not escape unscathed from serious trials. The disturbing memories remain."
— Hon. John C. Major, CC QC,
Justice of the Supreme Court of Canada.

Tough Crimes is a collection of thoughtful and insightful essays from some of Canada's most prominent criminal lawyers. Stories include wrongful convictions, reasonable doubt, homicides, and community spirit.

A percentage of book sales goes to World ORT, Education Program

Price: $29.95 *Trade Paperback*
288 pages

ISBN: 978-0-9689754-6-6 (2014)
E-book: 978-0-9689754-7-3 (2015)
Audio: 978-0-9689754-7-3 (2017)

SHRUNK: Crime and Disorders of the Mind
By J. Thomas Dalby *et al*
Book 2 in the True Cases Series

Foreword by Lisa Ramshaw
Edited by Lorene Shyba & J. Thomas Dalby

"The workings of the criminally disordered minds has always been a fascinating subject. Does our prison system throw away the key after incarceration or is it worthwhile to rehabilitate?"
— Earl Levy, QC

SHRUNK is a collection of true cases by eminent Canadian and international forensic psychologists and psychiatrists facing the tough topic of mental illness in the criminal justice system.

A percentage of book sales goes to The Canadian Schizophrenia Society.

Price: $29.95 *Trade Paperback*
274 pages

ISBN: 978-0-9947352-0-1 (2016)
E-book: 978-0-9947352-3-2 (2016)
Audio: 978-0-9952322-7-3 (2017)

Books in the Durvile 'True Cases' Legal Series

More Tough Crimes:
True Cases by Canadian Judges and Criminal Lawyers
By Donald Bayne *et al*
Book 3 in the True Cases Series

Foreword by Hon. Patrick LeSage
Edited by William Trudell & Lorene Shyba

"A revealing, at times searing and always very human look inside our criminal courtrooms and the people who populate them."

— Sean Fine, Globe and Mail

The third book in the "True Cases" series, *More Tough Crimes* provides readers with a window into the insightful thinking of some of Canada's best legal minds from coast to coast.

A percentage of book sales goes to Ikwe Widdjiitiwin Women's Shelter

Price: $29.95 *Trade Paperback*
274 pages

ISBN: 978-0-994735-2-56 (2017)
E-book: 978-0-9952322-2-8 (2017)
Audio: 978-0-9952322-9-7 (2018)

Women in Criminal Justice
True Cases By and About Canadian Women and the Law
By Susan Lang *et al*
Book 4 in the True Cases Series

Foreword by Rt. Hon. Beverley McLachlin
Edited by William Trudell & Lorene Shyba

The fourth book in the "True Cases" series, *Women in Criminal Justice* presents the perspectives of eminent Canadian judges and lawyers on urgent issues of our times. Topics include terrorism, drugs, sexual assault, mental disorders, motherhood, child protection, LGBTQ+, immigration, and Indigenous reconciliation.

A percentage of book sales goes to NWT Literary Council

Price: $29.95 *Trade Paperback*
274 pages

ISBN: 978-0-9947352-4-9 (2018)
E-book: 978-1-988824-14-7 (2018)
Audio: 978-1-988824-15-4 (2018)

Books in the 'Reflections' Series

Benched: Passion for Law Reform

By Hon. Nancy Morrison

Fifty years in a law profession she loves, 24 spent as a judge, Nancy Morrison is a great storyteller. Entertaining, at times warm and witty, this memoir also reminds us of dark days and tough social issues. With family roots in the Maritimes and prairies, Nancy's career spanned three provinces and two territories as a lawyer, arbitrator and judge.

Price: $29.95 *Trade Paperback*
ISBN: 978-1-988824-13-0 (Nov. 2018)

Eyepiece: Adventures in Canadian Film and Television

By Vic Sarin
Foreword by Rt. Hon. Adrienne Clarkson

"Sarin's rollicking recollections belong on the bookshelf of any serious aficionado of Canadian film history."
— Charlie Smith, Georgia Straight

In *Eyepiece* brilliant cinematographer and filmmaker Vic Sarin lays out the landscape of his over-150 documentary and dramatic films.

Price: $35.00 *Trade Paperback*
ISBN: 978-1-988824-02-4 (2017)

Milt Harradence: The Western Flair

Foreword by Hon. John C. Major, CC QC
Retired Justice, Supreme Court of Canada

"It should find a permanent home in every trial lawyer's library."
— Ron MacIsaac, Lawyers Weekly

In Milt Harradence: The Western Flair, C.D. Evans perpetuates the legend of his flamboyant, larger-than-life colleague with whom he shared thrills, spills, brilliant courtroom spars.

Price: $30.00 *Trade Paperback*
16 pages of colour photos.
ISBN: 978-0-9689754-0-4 (2000)

A Painful Duty
40 Years at the Criminal Bar

By C.D. Evans

"Very rarely have I read a memoir or autobiography whose author had as overwhelming concern for truth and fairness as Evans displays in this book."
— Alex Rettie, Alberta Views

Evans reveals insights into the practice and the characters of the Criminal Bar, with special tributes to no-nonsense judges.

Price: $42.50 *Trade Paperback*
16 pages of colour photos.
ISBN: 978-0-9689754-3-5 (2010)

Less Painful Duties
Reflections on the Revolution in the Legal Profession
By C.D. Evans

"It's a pleasure to hear somebody who knows what he's talking about find fault with the aspects of the justice system that are generally treated with white-gloved piety."
— Alex Rettie, Alberta Views

Evans reflects on topics such as the ascendancy of women in the profession, the *Canadian Charter of Rights*, and the impacts of technology.

Price: $29.95 *Trade Paperback*
ISBN: 978-0-9952322-1-1 (2017)

UpRoute Books and Media
Series Highlights

The Big Secret Book: An Intense Guide for Creating Performance Theatre

By Denise Clarke
Foreword by John Murrell

The Big Secret Book motivates and initiates creative abilities in performance creation. Written by Denise Clarke, director of One Yellow Rabbit Summer Lab Intensive, each chapter highlights aspects of the master class. Rich with visual images, the book also has sidebar sections providing glimpses of Clarke's genius in character development.

Price: $29.95 *Trade Paperback*
ISBN: 978-1-988824-11-6 (Nov. 2018)

Living in the Tall Grass
Poems of Reconciliation

By Chief R. Stacey Laforme
Book 2 in the Every River Poems Series

"An amazing collection of poems that serves to inspire ... Chief Laformes' poems are haunting and thought provoking ."
— Carrie MacKenzie, Anishinabek News

Through stories and poetry, Chief Laforme lets Canadians see through the eyes of Indigenous People. He says, "We should not have to change to fit into society, the world should change to embrace our uniqueness."

Price: $19.95 *Trade Paperback*
ISBN: 978-1-988824-05-05 (2018)

The Tree By the Woodpile and other Dene Spirit of Nature Tales

By Raymond Yakeleya
Book 1 in the Spirit of Nature Youth Series

"Raymond Yakeleya is among Indigenous people taking control of messaging in interesting ways."
— Carrie Tait, The Globe and Mail

The Tree by the Woodpile is about a Dene First Nations boy who is told enchanting tales by his elders, including how a tree provides food and shelter for animals of the North.

Youth, Ages 8-12
Price: $16.95 *Trade Paperback*
ISBN: 978-1-988824-03-1 (2018)

Stop Making Art and Die
Survival Activities for Artists

By Rich Théroux

"Stop Making Art and Die asks big questions about creativity, fulfillment, and happiness."
— Eric Volmers, Calgary Herald

The first adult activity book that makes it impossible not to succeed and flourish as and artist by encouraging a deeper understand of art.

Price: $24.95 *Trade Paperback*
ISBN: 978-0-9947352-2-5 (2015)

Shadow Hymns Photography by Austin Andrews

"There is power in the everyday scenes that often speak about reality, hardships, and the inspiring reliance of the people Andrews shoots."
— Eric Volmers, Calgary Herald

Shadow Hymns is an exploration of photojournalism by filmmaker Austin Andrews. Austin has profiled stories on six continents for *TIME, Foreign Policy, Macleans, Intersection,* and in the online edition of *National Geographic.*

Price: $29.95 *Trade Paperback*
Full-colour plates
ISBN: 978-1-988824-06-2 (2017)

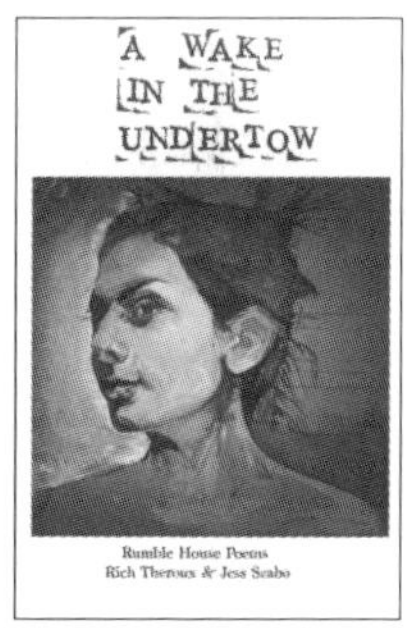

A Wake in the Undertow
Rumble House Poems

By Rich Theroux and Jess Szabo
Book 1 in the Every River Poems Series

A Wake in the Undertow contains poems from the creative spirits behind Calgary's Rumble House. Illustrated with enchanting drawings, the collection unveils people in love as they disclose things survived, dig deep for sacred weapons, and endure cantankerously, running on fumes.

Price: $19.95 *Trade Paperback*
ISBN: 978-0-9952322-4-2 (2016)